Unyielding Spirit

Mastering the Mind: The Young Athlete's Guide to Developing Mental Toughness and Resilience

Connor Langley

Summary

Chapter 1: Introduction to Mental Mastery in Sports

Sports have always been a captivating and essential part of human culture. From the ancient Olympics in Greece to the contemporary world of professional athletics, sports have constantly tested the limits of human capabilities. Athletes have pushed their physical boundaries, achieving incredible feats of strength, speed, and endurance. However, behind these outstanding physical accomplishments lies a crucial element that often goes unnoticed - the power of the mind. In this chapter, we will delve into the world of mental mastery in sports, exploring how a strong mental game can be the key to unlocking an athlete's full potential.

The Mind-Body Connection

It is widely acknowledged that sports require a harmony between the mind and body. While physical training strengthens the body, mental mastery allows athletes to tap into their full power. The mind-body connection is a fundamental aspect of athletic performance, as success in any sport heavily relies on mental resilience, focus, and determination. In fact, research has consistently shown that elite athletes can outperform their competitors due to superior mental fortitude.

Understanding the Power of the Mind

To fully comprehend the role of the mind in sports, it is crucial to understand the various components that contribute to mental mastery. First and foremost is self-awareness - recognizing one's strengths, weaknesses, and emotional responses. By acknowledging these factors, athletes can better manage their thoughts, emotions, and behaviors in highly competitive situations.

Secondly, mental visualization plays a pivotal role in an athlete's performance. By mentally rehearsing different scenarios, athletes can improve their decision-making abilities and motor skills. Visualization helps them create a mental blueprint for success, boosting their confidence and optimizing their performance.

Thirdly, the art of setting goals and maintaining focus is vital in the pursuit of excellence. Athletes who set well-defined goals have a clear vision of what they want to accomplish, and their focused mindset enables them to persevere through challenges and setbacks. Goal setting facilitates the creation of a roadmap to success, providing athletes with a sense of purpose and direction.

Controlling Negative Thoughts

Negative thoughts can be like stumbling blocks, hindering an athlete's progress and sabotaging their performance. Therefore, mental mastery involves learning effective techniques to manage negative self-talk and doubts. By engaging in positive self-affirmations, athletes can shift their mindset from self-doubt to self-belief. Moreover, utilizing mindfulness techniques such as deep breathing and meditation can help athletes regain focus in moments of stress or distraction.

Managing Pre-Competition Anxiety

Pre-competition anxiety is a common phenomenon experienced by athletes across all disciplines. The fear of failure, the anticipation of success, and the pressure to perform at one's best can all contribute to heightened anxiety levels. Mental mastery empowers athletes to conquer these anxieties by implementing relaxation techniques, developing pre-competition routines, and maintaining a confident mindset.

Building Resilience

One of the most significant aspects of mental mastery in sports is the development of resilience. Resilience enables athletes to bounce back from setbacks, persevere through challenges, and remain motivated despite adversity. It is through resilience that champions emerge. By cultivating mental toughness and the ability to adapt to changing circumstances, athletes can elevate their performance to new heights.

The Role of Mental Mastery in Different Sports

While the importance of mental mastery applies to all sports, certain disciplines place a premium on different aspects of mental training. In team sports like basketball or soccer, communication, teamwork, and mental composure during high-pressure moments are essential. Individual sports such as tennis or golf may require intense focus, the ability to control emotions, and the capacity to overcome the inherent solitude of competition.

This chapter has provided a comprehensive overview of the concept of mental mastery in sports. Understanding the mind-body connection, harnessing the power of the mind, and learning to control negative thoughts and anxiety are all crucial components of an athlete's mental game. By developing mental resilience, athletes can overcome setbacks, push through challenges, and unlock their full potential. In the subsequent chapters of this book, we will delve deeper into specific mental training techniques and strategies to help athletes maximize their performance in their respective sports.

The Crucial Role of the Mind in Athletic Performance: Overview of the intertwined relationship between physical and mental strength

Athletic performance is not solely determined by physical prowess; it is also influenced significantly by the power of the mind. Athletes who achieve greatness often possess a unique blend of physical abilities, mental fortitude, and psychological resilience. In this chapter, we delve into the essential role the mind plays in athletic performance, exploring the intricacies of the intertwined relationship between physical and mental strength.

1. Mental Preparation and Focus:

One of the key factors determining success in sports is an athlete's ability to prepare mentally for competition. Mental preparation encompasses a range of techniques, such as visualization, goal setting, self-talk, and mindfulness. Visualization, or mentally rehearsing specific movements and scenarios, helps athletes enhance their kinesthetic awareness and improve performance. Goal setting, both short-term and long-term, provides athletes with a clear direction and establishes a framework for focused training. Moreover, self-talk, the internal dialogue athletes engage in during practice and competition, can have a profound impact on their confidence and ability to overcome challenges. Finally, mindfulness, the practice of present-moment awareness, helps athletes stay centered, reduce distractions, and maintain focus during high-pressure situations.

2. Controlling Performance Anxiety:

Performance anxiety can be debilitating for athletes, resulting in decreased confidence, impaired decision-making, and inferior execution of skills. Managing anxiety is crucial for optimal athletic performance. Techniques such as deep breathing, progressive muscle relaxation, and cognitive restructuring empower athletes to regulate their anxiety levels effectively. Deep breathing helps activate the body's relaxation response, counteracting the harmful effects of anxiety. Progressive muscle relaxation involves tensing and then intentionally releasing each muscle group, leading to physical and mental tension reduction. Cognitive restructuring, on the other hand, involves reframing negative thoughts and replacing them with positive, constructive alternatives, fostering resilience and promoting better performance.

3. Building Mental Resilience:

Athletes encounter numerous setbacks and obstacles throughout their careers, making mental resilience indispensable. Developing mental resilience involves cultivating a growth mindset, embracing challenges, learning from failure, and harnessing motivation. A growth mindset acknowledges that skills can be developed through hard work and dedication, thus enabling athletes to view setbacks as opportunities for growth rather than indicators of failure. Embracing challenges allows athletes to step out of their comfort zones, pushing their physical and mental limits, and ultimately achieving greater success. Learning from failure involves extracting valuable lessons from past mistakes or losses, fueling personal growth and improvement. Lastly, harnessing motivation enables athletes to maintain their drive, passion, and commitment, even when faced with adversity or fatigue.

4. Psychological Techniques for Performance Enhancement:
Numerous psychological techniques can directly enhance an athlete's performance. These techniques include positive imagery, positive self-talk, attentional focus, and mental rehearsal. Positive imagery involves picturing successful performances and outcomes, bolstering confidence and motivation. Positive self-talk entails using affirmative, constructive language to cultivate optimism and belief in oneself. Attentional focus refers to maintaining concentration on relevant cues and blocking out distractions, optimizing an athlete's ability to make split-second decisions and execute precise skills. Mental rehearsal, often used in combination with visualization, allows athletes to mentally practice particular movements, strategies, or scenarios, enhancing their overall performance.

5. The Impact of Emotional Intelligence:
Emotional intelligence, the ability to recognize, understand, and regulate one's own and others' emotions, plays an integral role in athletic performance. Athletes with high emotional intelligence can effectively manage emotions such as anger, frustration, and anxiety,

enabling them to stay focused and composed during competition. Moreover, emotional intelligence facilitates effective communication and team dynamics, as athletes with this trait can empathize with teammates, understand their emotions better, and build strong interpersonal relationships. The cultivation of emotional intelligence empowers athletes to harness their emotions as allies instead of being controlled by them, leading to improved overall performance.

Understanding the indispensable role of the mind in athletic performance is vital for both athletes and coaches alike. By acknowledging the intertwined relationship between physical and mental strength, athletes can unlock their full potential and achieve greatness. Mental preparedness, the ability to control performance anxiety, building mental resilience, employing psychological techniques for performance enhancement, and fostering emotional intelligence are all essential components of the athlete's journey towards excellence. Through continued exploration, understanding, and application of these concepts, athletes can maximize their performance and thrive in their respective sports.

The Unyielding Spirit of Champions: Case studies of iconic athletes who showcased unparalleled mental toughness.

In the world of sports, where the line between victory and defeat is often razor-thin, there are certain individuals who transcend the bounds of physical ability and demonstrate an unyielding spirit that sets them apart from their peers. These iconic athletes possess a mental prowess that enables them to overcome insurmountable obstacles, push beyond their limits, and emerge as champions. In this chapter, we delve into the lives and careers of three such individuals, showcasing their remarkable mental toughness and the lessons we can learn from their extraordinary journeys.

Case Study 1: Muhammad Ali - The Greatest of All Time

Muhammad Ali, widely regarded as one of the greatest boxers in history, exemplified the unyielding spirit of a champion both inside and outside the ring. From brash self-confidence to humanitarian efforts, Ali's mental toughness was unrivaled.

Ali's mental fortitude was on display during his famous "Rumble in the Jungle" fight against George Foreman in 1974. The odds were heavily stacked against Ali, as Foreman was unbeaten and considered an unstoppable force. Despite this, Ali devised a strategy known as the "rope-a-dope," allowing Foreman to tire himself out by relentlessly pounding Ali's defense.

This tactic not only showcased Ali's physical endurance but also highlighted his unwavering belief in his abilities. Ali embraced the pain, weathered the storm of Foreman's powerful blows, and ultimately knocked out his opponent, securing an improbable victory.

Outside the ring, Ali's unyielding spirit was evident in his relentless activism, particularly during the Vietnam War. Defying societal expectations and risking his career, Ali steadfastly refused induction into the military, citing his religious beliefs and opposition to the war. His unwavering stance caused a rift in the nation but also garnered respect for his unyielding spirit.

Ali's ability to navigate adversity while staying true to his beliefs is one of the ultimate displays of mental toughness. His legacy continues to inspire generations of athletes to tap into their own untapped reserves of strength and determination.

Case Study 2: Serena Williams - Defying the Odds

Serena Williams, the dominant force in women's tennis during the 21st century, is a prime example of an athlete who consistently exhibited unparalleled mental toughness. Her journey to the top was paved with obstacles, but her unyielding spirit propelled her to become one of the greatest sports icons of all time.

From a young age, Williams faced criticism and discrimination due to her race, gender, and unconventional playing style. Instead of letting these challenges break her spirit, she used them as fuel to drive her forward. Williams' mental toughness allowed her to silence her naysayers and develop a never-give-up attitude that became her trademark.

One of the most memorable displays of Williams' resilience came during the 2017 Australian Open. Battling health issues, a difficult childbirth, and the long road to recovery, Williams returned to the tennis court as an underdog. Despite the odds stacked against her, she refused to succumb to self-doubt, channeling her mental fortitude to reach the finals. Although she fell short of winning the championship, her journey was truly awe-inspiring, leaving an indelible mark on the tennis world.

Williams' unyielding spirit extends beyond her individual success on the court. Throughout her career, she has been a powerful advocate for equality and social justice, consistently using her platform to raise awareness and inspire change. Her unwavering commitment to fighting for what she believes in is a testament to her extraordinary mental toughness.

Case Study 3: Michael Jordan - The Relentless Competitor

No discussion of mental toughness in the world of sports is complete without mentioning Michael Jordan. The basketball legend's unmatched drive, competitiveness, and unyielding spirit earned him numerous accolades and universal recognition as one of the greatest athletes of all time.

Jordan's mental toughness was perhaps best showcased in the 1997 NBA Finals. Battling a severe flu, commonly referred to as the "Flu Game," Jordan delivered an awe-inspiring performance. Despite his ailing physical condition, he scored 38 points, leading his team to victory. Jordan's ability to push through his physical limitations and perform at the highest level illustrated his unparalleled mental fortitude.

Beyond his on-court success, Jordan's tenacity was evident in his relentless pursuit of greatness. He famously stated, "I've failed over and over and over again in my life, and that is why I succeed." Jordan's unyielding spirit enabled him to bounce back from setbacks, learn from failures, and ultimately become an unstoppable force in basketball.

The unyielding spirit demonstrated by Muhammad Ali, Serena Williams, and Michael Jordan serves as an inspiration for athletes across the globe. These iconic individuals remind us that success goes beyond physical prowess; it requires unwavering mental toughness, resilience, and an indomitable spirit. As we delve deeper into the chapters ahead, we will explore the key lessons we can learn from their journeys and the strategies we can implement to cultivate our own unyielding spirit, both on and off the field.

Defining Mental Toughness and Resilience: A deeper look into what these concepts truly mean

In the realm of personal development and achieving success, two concepts have gained significant attention and praise: mental toughness and resilience. These terms are often used interchangeably, but what do they truly mean? Are mental toughness and resilience just buzzwords thrown around in self-help books and seminars, or do they possess deeper significance? In this chapter, we will delve into the essence of mental toughness and resilience, exploring their definitions, components, and the crucial role they play in our lives.

Defining Mental Toughness

Mental toughness is commonly misunderstood as merely having a thick skin or an ability to persevere through difficult situations. However, it encompasses a broader spectrum of qualities and mindset that enable individuals to overcome challenges with unwavering determination.

At its core, mental toughness refers to an individual's ability to adapt, persevere, and remain focused in the face of adversity. It involves developing a resilient mindset that empowers individuals to effectively deal with stress, setbacks, and obstacles. Mental toughness goes beyond physical endurance; it involves mental and emotional strength, allowing individuals to maintain peak performance while under pressure.

Components of Mental Toughness

To understand the true essence of mental toughness, we must explore its fundamental components:

1. Emotional Control: Mental toughness requires individuals to regulate their emotions effectively. It involves recognizing and managing negative emotions such as fear, anger, and anxiety, while maintaining a positive and optimistic outlook.

2. Confidence: Believing in oneself is a cornerstone of mental toughness. Individuals with this trait trust their abilities and judgment, allowing them to take risks and face challenges head-on.

3. Optimal Focus: Mental toughness necessitates the ability to concentrate and stay fully engaged in the present moment, despite distractions or potentially overwhelming circumstances. This focus ensures individuals maintain clarity and make sound decisions even in high-pressure situations.

4. Resilience: A resilient mindset serves as the backbone of mental toughness. It involves bouncing back from setbacks, failures, and

disappointments, ultimately fueling personal growth and determination.

Defining Resilience

While mental toughness equips individuals to tackle challenges head-on, resilience pertains to the ability to recover and bounce back from adversity. Resilience allows individuals to embrace life's difficulties, adapt to change, and maintain their mental and emotional well-being throughout tumultuous times.

Resilience encompasses not only the fundamental skill of bouncing back but also the ability to learn from adversity and grow stronger as a result. It involves cultivating psychological strength and flexibility to successfully navigate difficult circumstances, personal setbacks, and even traumatic events.

Components of Resilience

To gain a deeper understanding of resilience, we must examine its key components:

1. Emotional Regulation: Resilience requires individuals to manage and process emotions effectively. Emotional regulation allows individuals to confront and accept their feelings without being overwhelmed, enabling them to successfully adapt to challenging situations.

2. Self-Reflection: Resilience is built upon the ability to reflect upon experiences and learn from them. By understanding their reactions, motivations, and thought processes, individuals can develop a clearer sense of self-awareness, which aids in cultivating resilience.

3. Social Support Networks: A significant aspect of resilience is the availability of a support system. Surrounding oneself with positive and empathetic individuals contributes to resilience, as it provides emotional support, guidance, and helps cultivate a sense of belonging.

4. Positive Mindset: Maintaining an optimistic outlook encourages resilience. A positive mindset allows individuals to see setbacks and challenges as opportunities for growth and personal development, rather than insurmountable obstacles.

The Interplay between Mental Toughness and Resilience

Mental toughness and resilience are not stand-alone concepts; they are inherently interconnected. Mental toughness provides individuals with the tools and mindset necessary to confront adversity, while resilience empowers them to recover, grow, and thrive in the face of challenges.

Without mental toughness, individuals may struggle to face obstacles head-on and may fall victim to feelings of helplessness or self-doubt. On the other hand, without resilience, mental toughness alone may lead to burnout and a lack of personal growth, as individuals can become rigid and resistant to change.

Together, mental toughness and resilience create a powerful synergy, enabling individuals to maintain peak performance, thrive in adversity, and seize opportunities for personal development and growth.

In this chapter, we have explored the depths of mental toughness and resilience, unraveling their true meanings and significance. Mental toughness encompasses emotional control, confidence, optimal focus, and resilience, allowing individuals to adapt and persevere through adversity. Resilience, on the other hand, encompasses emotional regulation, self-reflection, social support networks, and a positive mindset, enabling individuals to bounce back from setbacks and grow stronger.

Mental toughness and resilience are not just buzzwords; they epitomize the essence of personal development, allowing individuals to transform their lives by embracing challenges, developing unwavering determination, and cultivating psychological strength. By understanding the interplay between mental toughness and resilience, individuals can embark on a journey towards self-mastery, achieving success and personal fulfillment in every facet of life.

The Young Athlete's Mental Landscape: Understanding the unique challenges and pressures young athletes face

Sports play a significant role in the lives of young athletes, providing opportunities for physical activity, personal growth, and valuable life lessons. However, behind the glitz and glory of sports, lies the often overlooked mental landscape that young athletes must navigate. This chapter aims to shed light on the unique challenges and pressures young athletes face, offering insights into their mental well-being and helping stakeholders develop a holistic approach towards their development.

Defining the Young Athlete's Mental Landscape:

The mental landscape of a young athlete encompasses various psychological factors that influence their performance, self-esteem, motivation, and overall mental well-being. It involves a complex interplay of emotions, beliefs, expectations, and coping mechanisms, all of which can profoundly impact their athletic journey. Recognizing and understanding these elements is crucial for coaches, parents, and all involved in supporting young athletes.

1. Developing Self-Identity:

For young athletes, sports provide an avenue to form their self-identity. The achievement of success in their respective sports becomes intertwined with their sense of self-worth. When triumphs and failures become indicators of personal value, it places immense pressure on them to perform consistently and meet external expectations. It is essential for stakeholders to foster a healthy self-identity, focusing on character development, values, and intrinsic motivation.

2. Balancing Multiple Roles:

Young athletes often find themselves juggling multiple roles, from being a student, sibling, friend, to being an athlete. Society's demand for excellence in all aspects of life can overwhelm them, leaving little room for individual growth and self-discovery. The pressure to excel academically while maintaining peak physical performance can adversely affect their mental well-being. It is crucial for adults to support and guide young athletes in finding a balance between their different roles without compromising their mental health.

3. Dealing with Failure:

Failure is an inevitable part of sports, and young athletes are not spared from it. Whether it's losing a match or failing to achieve a personal goal, these setbacks can have a profound impact on their psyche. Young athletes are often in a vulnerable state, struggling to cope with disappointment and fear of judgment. It is vital for coaches and parents to help them develop resilience, emphasizing the importance of learning from failure and using it as a catalyst for growth.

4. Performance Anxiety:

The competitive nature of sports can lead to heightened performance anxiety in young athletes. From pre-game nerves to fear of making mistakes, anxiety can impede their performance and erode their enjoyment of the sport. Helping young athletes manage their anxiety through relaxation techniques, positive self-talk, and mental skills training can not only enhance their performance but also promote their overall mental well-being.

5. Coping with Pressure:

External pressure, whether from coaches, parents, or peers, adds an additional layer of complexity to the young athlete's mental landscape. Expectations to win, secure scholarships, or achieve professional careers can be overwhelming, leading to elevated stress levels. Establishing clear lines of communication and creating a supportive environment wherein athletes feel safe to express their concerns can help alleviate some of the pressure they experience.

6. Maintaining a Healthy Body Image:

Sports often place great emphasis on physical appearance and athleticism. Young athletes can easily succumb to societal pressures, leading to body image concerns and disordered eating patterns.

Coaches and parents must promote a healthy body image, focusing on performance rather than external appearance. Ensuring that athletes have access to proper nutrition education and support can prevent the development of harmful habits.

7. Managing Time and Burnout:

The demanding schedule of young athletes, with extensive training sessions and frequent competitions, can take a toll on their mental health. Balancing academic responsibilities, social engagements, and physical exertion can lead to exhaustion and burnout. Recognizing the importance of rest and recovery, along with emphasizing time management skills, allows young athletes to maintain a healthy relationship with their sports and avoid overexertion.

Understanding the intricacies of a young athlete's mental landscape is crucial for their well-being and development. By acknowledging the unique challenges and pressures they face, stakeholders can provide appropriate support and guidance. Creating a nurturing environment that fosters resilience, self-discovery, and a healthy balance between sports and other aspects of life will empower young athletes to navigate their mental landscape with confidence. By addressing their mental well-being alongside physical training, we can ensure that young athletes flourish not only as performers but also as healthy, fulfilled individuals.

Chapter 2: The Foundations of Mental Toughness

In the realm of personal development, mental toughness stands as a formidable quality that greatly influences an individual's ability to overcome challenges, achieve goals, and thrive in the face of adversity. It is a trait that transcends mere physical strength, as it is primarily rooted in mindset, emotional resilience, and unwavering determination. In this chapter, we delve deep into the foundations of mental toughness, understanding its importance, characteristics, and how one can cultivate it to enhance their personal and professional lives.

The Meaning of Mental Toughness:

At its core, mental toughness refers to the ability to adapt, withstand, and recover from stress, pressure, and setbacks. It encompasses having a growth-oriented mindset, emotional intelligence, and an indomitable spirit. Mental toughness equips individuals with the resilience to persist in the face of obstacles, maintain focus, and thrive amidst uncertainty. While some people may seem naturally mentally tough, it is a skill that can be built and honed with intentional effort and practice.

Characteristics of Mental Toughness:

1. Purpose and Clarity:

Individuals possessing mental toughness have a clear sense of purpose and direction. They set goals that challenge them and align with their values and passions. Having a strong sense of purpose provides the needed motivation during challenging times, helping to navigate through obstacles and sustain resilience.

2. Positive Mindset:

Mentally tough individuals have a positive outlook on life, even in the face of difficulties. They embrace challenges as opportunities for growth and see setbacks as temporary hurdles rather than permanent failures. They understand that negativity only hampers progress and actively cultivate a mindset that focuses on possibilities, solutions, and gratitude.

3. Resilience:

Resilience is the cornerstone of mental toughness. It is the ability to bounce back from setbacks, adapt to change, and remain optimistic. Mentally tough individuals see setbacks as learning opportunities, allowing them to grow stronger and smarter. They embrace failure as an essential part of the journey towards success, refusing to let it define them or diminish their self-belief.

4. Emotional Intelligence:

Mental toughness goes beyond sheer willpower; it involves

understanding and managing one's emotions effectively. Emotionally intelligent individuals have a heightened self-awareness, allowing them to recognize and regulate their emotions constructively. They also possess the ability to empathize with others, which helps foster better relationships and enables effective collaboration.

5. Discipline and Self-Control:

Mentally tough individuals exhibit high levels of self-discipline. They possess the ability to delay gratification, make difficult choices, and stay focused on their long-term goals. They resist distractions and temptations to maintain their commitment and drive towards success. Their self-control allows them to consistently make choices that align with their values and priorities.

6. Optimism and Positivity:

Positivity is a key characteristic of mental toughness. Optimistic individuals believe in their ability to overcome challenges, viewing setbacks as temporary roadblocks rather than insurmountable barriers. They find the silver lining in difficult situations and maintain an unwavering hope for a better future. This positivity acts as a fuel that propels them forward.

Cultivating Mental Toughness:

Now that we have explored the essential components of mental toughness, let's delve into practical strategies to cultivate this invaluable trait:

1. Practice Mindfulness:

Mindfulness is a practice that involves being fully present in the current moment, without judgment or attachment. By training yourself to focus on the present, you build resilience and reduce the influence of external stressors. Regular mindfulness exercises, such as meditation or deep breathing, can help you develop a calm and centered mindset essential for mental toughness.

2. Set Challenging Goals:

Setting challenging, yet achievable, goals is crucial for developing mental toughness. These goals should be aligned with your passion and values, helping to fuel your motivation and persistence. Break them down into smaller, manageable steps, allowing you to track your progress and celebrate victories along the way. Each small success will boost your confidence and reinforce your mental resilience.

3. Embrace Discomfort:

Mental toughness requires pushing beyond the boundaries of your comfort zone. Embracing discomfort builds resilience and expands your capabilities. Engage in activities that challenge you and force you to confront fears or insecurities. By willingly stepping into discomfort, you train yourself to manage stress, heighten focus, and persevere in high-pressure situations.

4. Cultivate a Growth Mindset:

Adopting a growth mindset involves believing that abilities and intelligence can be developed through effort and perseverance.

Embrace challenges as opportunities to learn and grow, rather than avoid them due to fear of failure. Emphasize the process of acquiring knowledge and skills, rather than solely focusing on outcomes. This mindset shift fosters resilience, allowing setbacks to propel you forward rather than impede your progress.

5. Build a Supportive Network:

Surrounding yourself with like-minded individuals who share your values and growth-oriented mindset is crucial for cultivating mental toughness. Seek out individuals who inspire and challenge you to reach new heights. Engage in meaningful conversations, share experiences, and support each other in times of difficulty. A strong support network provides the encouragement and accountability necessary for continuous growth.

The foundations of mental toughness are essential for personal and professional success. By developing purpose and clarity, cultivating a positive mindset, embracing resilience, enhancing emotional intelligence, practicing discipline and self-control, and fostering optimism, one can build unwavering mental toughness. With perseverance and intentional effort, mental toughness becomes an invaluable asset that unlocks your potential, enables you to overcome challenges, and propels you towards achieving your aspirations.

Building Mental Stamina from Scratch: Steps to start strengthening one's mental fortitude.

In our fast-paced and demanding modern world, mental strength has become a crucial asset. The ability to face challenges head-on, persevere through adversity, and maintain a positive mindset is essential for success and personal well-being. However, developing mental stamina is not an overnight process; it requires dedication, practice, and strategic steps. In this chapter, we will explore the fundamental strategies and exercises to kick-start your journey toward building mental fortitude.

Understanding Mental Stamina

Before diving into the steps to enhance your mental resilience, it is essential to grasp the concept of mental stamina. Mental stamina refers to the ability to endure psychological challenges, setbacks, and stressors without losing focus, motivation, or composure. It involves developing resilience, emotional stability, and a strong mindset. Just as physical fitness requires regular exercise and training, mental stamina demands consistent effort and practice to overcome obstacles and setbacks.

Step 1: Cultivate a Growth Mindset

The first step toward building mental stamina is cultivating a growth mindset. A growth mindset views challenges and failures as opportunities for growth and learning, rather than setbacks.

Embrace the belief that your abilities and intelligence can be developed through dedication, effort, and continuous learning. Adopting a growth mindset allows you to approach challenges with optimism and the willingness to persevere through difficulties, ultimately strengthening your mental stamina.

To cultivate a growth mindset, train yourself to reframe negative thoughts and self-doubt into positive ones. Challenge your own fixed beliefs about your abilities and possibilities. Acknowledge that your potential is not predetermined and that improvement is always possible through effort and perseverance. By embracing a growth mindset, you lay the foundation for building mental strength.

Step 2: Practice Resilience through Adversity

Resilience is a vital trait in building mental stamina. It is the ability to bounce back from setbacks, adapt to change, and remain emotionally stable in the face of adversity. Resilience is strengthened through exposure to challenging situations and actively practicing strategies to overcome them.

Setbacks and failures are inevitable in life, but they also provide valuable opportunities for growth. Embrace these challenges rather than avoiding them, as they can serve as stepping stones to develop resilience. Reflect on past experiences and identify the lessons learned from overcoming adversity. Work on establishing a positive relationship with failure, viewing it as an opportunity for growth and self-improvement.

To practice resilience, intentionally put yourself in uncomfortable situations and gradually increase the difficulty of these challenges. This could involve taking on new responsibilities, learning new skills, or stepping out of your comfort zone. By exposing yourself to adversity and intentionally building resilience, you will enhance your mental stamina.

Step 3: Develop Emotional Intelligence
Emotional intelligence plays a significant role in building mental fortitude. It involves the ability to recognize, understand, and manage your emotions effectively, as well as empathize with others. Developing emotional intelligence enables you to regulate your emotions, navigate conflicts efficiently, and maintain a positive mindset.

Start by becoming more aware of your emotions and their triggers. Practice mindfulness and self-reflection to recognize and understand your emotional patterns. Take time to process your feelings and find healthy ways to express them. Engage in activities such as journaling or talking to a trusted friend or therapist to enhance your emotional self-awareness.

Additionally, work on deepening your empathetic skills. Seek to understand others' perspectives, listen actively, and practice empathy in your daily interactions. Developing emotional intelligence will provide you with the tools to handle stress, manage challenging situations, and develop a more resilient mindset.

Step 4: Build a Supportive Network

In your journey to strengthen mental stamina, having a supportive network is essential. Surround yourself with individuals who motivate, inspire, and uplift you. Seek out like-minded individuals who are also striving for personal growth and mental resilience. Sharing experiences and challenges with others can provide valuable insights and support.

Build relationships that will encourage and hold you accountable on your journey. Engage in open and honest conversations, share your goals, and seek advice from trusted individuals who have already demonstrated mental fortitude in their own lives. A strong support system will help you stay focused and motivated, especially during difficult times.

Step 5: Adopt Healthy Habits

Building mental stamina requires a holistic approach that encompasses physical, emotional, and mental well-being. Adopting healthy habits will contribute to overall mental resilience. Ensure you prioritize self-care and engage in activities that promote mental health.

Exercise regularly to boost endorphin levels and reduce stress. A healthy body supports a healthy mind. Practice stress-reducing activities such as meditation, deep breathing exercises, or yoga. Engage in hobbies or activities that bring you joy and help you relax.

Additionally, prioritize quality sleep and maintain a balanced diet. Sleep deprivation and poor nutrition can impact your mood, cognitive function, and overall mental strength. By adopting healthy habits, you provide your body and mind with the necessary foundation to cultivate mental stamina.

Building mental stamina is a lifelong journey that requires consistent effort and practice. By cultivating a growth mindset, embracing challenges, developing emotional intelligence, building a support network, and adopting healthy habits, you can start strengthening your mental fortitude from scratch. Remember, mental resilience is not about avoiding difficulties but rather facing them head-on, growing through them, and emerging stronger than before. The steps outlined in this chapter will serve as a solid foundation for your ongoing pursuit of mental strength and well-being.

The Role of Discipline in the Athletic Mindset: How discipline can forge an ironclad spirit

In the realm of sports and athletics, discipline is the bedrock upon which success is built. It is the unyielding force that separates the average from the exceptional, the strong from the weak, and the winners from the losers. Discipline breeds character, resilience, and determination, ultimately forging an ironclad spirit within athletes that propels them to greatness. In this chapter, we will explore the pivotal role of discipline in the athletic mindset, delving into its various dimensions and how it can be harnessed to unlock untapped potential within athletes.

Discipline: The Foundation of Achievement:

At its core, discipline is the unwavering commitment to a set of principles, values, and standards, regardless of external circumstances. It is the steadfast adherence to a routine, sacrifice, and self-control, driven by an unrelenting desire for excellence. In the world of sports, discipline manifests itself in myriad ways, both on and off the field. From showing up to training sessions on time, following a strict diet plan, embracing rigorous workout regimens, to adhering to team strategies, every aspect of an athlete's life is intertwined with discipline.

Training the Mind: Mental Discipline:

While physical discipline is undoubtedly crucial in athletic pursuits, mental discipline is equally imperative. The ability to control one's thoughts, emotions, and reactions in high-pressure situations is a hallmark of a disciplined athlete. Psychological fortitude and focus are the result of years of practice and strict mental training. Athletes must learn to quiet self-doubt, block out distractions, and believe in their abilities, even when the odds are stacked against them. Cultivating mental discipline requires resilience, patience, and the willingness to confront and conquer one's fears.

Striving for Excellence: The Discipline of Continuous Improvement:

Discipline in the athletic mindset is synonymous with a never-ending pursuit of excellence. Athletes driven by discipline are insatiable learners, constantly seeking ways to refine their techniques, enhance their skills, and overcome their limitations. They embrace feedback, critique, and the discomfort of pushing beyond their comfort zones. In the face of setbacks and failures, disciplined individuals rise stronger, using each stumble as an opportunity to grow. Continuous improvement demands dedication, consistency, and a mindset that embraces challenges as stepping stones towards success.

Building Strong Habits: The Discipline of Routine:

Athletes are creatures of habit. The discipline of routine is an integral component of an athlete's success. By creating and adhering to a structured routine, athletes eliminate decision fatigue and channel their energies towards the pursuit of their goals. A disciplined routine allows athletes to optimize their physical and mental well-being, ensuring adequate rest, recovery, and preparation. From waking up at the crack of dawn for early morning runs to meticulously planning training sessions, top athletes understand the power of routine as the building block of success.

Resilience and Grit: The Discipline of Perseverance:

Athletics, by its very nature, is a crucible of adversity and challenges. In the face of setbacks, injuries, or defeats, disciplined athletes exhibit incomparable resilience and unyielding determination. They view every obstacle as an opportunity, refusing to succumb to defeat. The discipline of perseverance allows athletes to bounce back from disappointments, learn from failures, and emerge even stronger. It is through enduring difficulties that an athlete's spirit is tempered, forging an indomitable will that refuses to back down.

The Discipline of Teamwork:

While sports may often seem like individual pursuits, the role of discipline in teamwork cannot be undermined. Athletes who respect and understand the significance of teamwork embrace self-discipline to function effectively within a collective unit. They adhere to team strategies, communicate clearly, and prioritize the greater good over personal gain. The discipline of teamwork instills trust, camaraderie, and a shared sense of purpose, ultimately leading the team to achieve unprecedented heights.

Discipline serves as the cornerstone of the athletic mindset, shaping athletes into individuals capable of pushing their physical and mental boundaries. It instills qualities such as dedication, focus, resilience, and tenacity, which are essential for success in sports and life. The journey towards athletic excellence is paved with hardships, sacrifices, and countless hours of relentless work. Only those who embrace discipline as their guiding principle can hope to forge an ironclad spirit capable of withstanding the fiercest of challenges. As we continue our exploration of the athletic mindset, let us remember that discipline is not just a means to an end but a way of life for those who aspire to greatness.

Embracing Challenges as Opportunities: Shifting perspectives to face adversities head-on

Life is full of challenges, big and small. Some of these challenges may knock us down, leaving us feeling defeated and overwhelmed. However, if we can shift our perspective and see challenges as opportunities for growth and self-improvement, we can overcome adversities and create a path to greatness. In this chapter, we will delve deeper into the art of embracing challenges, understanding how shifting our perspectives can empower us to face adversities head-on and ultimately transform our lives.

The Power of Shifting Perspectives:

One of the greatest catalysts for personal growth is the ability to shift our perspectives. It allows us to view challenges as stepping stones rather than stumbling blocks. When we consciously choose to see adversities as opportunities, our mindsets change, opening up new doors for growth and transformation.

Imagine a young entrepreneur who has worked tirelessly on launching a new business venture, only to face a sudden financial setback. Rather than becoming disheartened and giving up, she chooses to see this challenge as an opportunity to learn and grow. By shifting her perspective, she embraces the setback, analyzes the situation, and identifies potential areas for improvement. This shift in perspective not only empowers her to overcome the financial setback but also equips her with the knowledge and skills to navigate future challenges.

Challenges as Gateways to Personal Development:

Every challenge we face is a unique opportunity for personal development. It is through challenges that we discover our true strengths, resilience, and capabilities. By embracing challenges, we tap into our potential and unlock the doors to personal growth.

Take the example of an aspiring writer facing rejection after rejection from publishers. Instead of succumbing to self-doubt and giving up on their dreams, they persevere and use each rejection as an opportunity for improvement. They seek feedback, refine their writing style, and develop a toolkit of skills essential for success. Eventually, their persistence pays off, and their manuscript finds a home with a publisher. This journey of embracing challenges not only improved their writing but also shaped their character and instilled within them a newfound sense of determination and resilience.

The Role of Mindset in Facing Challenges:

Our mindset plays a vital role in how we perceive and respond to challenges. A fixed mindset, characterized by the belief that our abilities are fixed and cannot be developed, fosters avoidance and a fear of failure. In contrast, a growth mindset, rooted in the belief that our abilities can be cultivated through effort and determination, empowers us to face challenges head-on.

Individuals with a growth mindset understand that challenges are opportunities to learn and grow, regardless of the outcome. They recognize that setbacks and failures are part of the journey towards success and embrace them as valuable learning experiences. With a growth mindset, they view challenges as a chance to push their boundaries, develop new skills, and discover untapped potential.

Cultivating a growth mindset requires conscious effort and self-reflection. It involves reframing negative self-talk, developing a sense of self-compassion, seeking challenges, and embracing the discomfort that accompanies growth. By nurturing a growth mindset, we empower ourselves to face challenges confidently, knowing that growth and success are within our reach.

Embracing Challenges in Relationships:

Challenges are not limited to individual pursuits; they also emerge within our relationships. Whether it be a strained friendship, a struggling marriage, or a difficult family dynamic, challenges in relationships provide an opportunity for introspection, growth, and deeper connections.

Let's consider a couple facing compatibility issues within their marriage. Instead of viewing these challenges as insurmountable barriers, they choose to see them as an opportunity to learn more about themselves and each other. Through couples therapy, open communication, and a willingness to grow individually and as a couple, they turn their challenges into meaningful and transformative experiences. By embracing the hardships, they strengthen their bond and develop a relationship built on trust, empathy, and shared growth.

Embracing challenges as opportunities requires a shift in perspective, a growth mindset, and a willingness to step outside of our comfort zones. By recognizing that challenges are not roadblocks, but rather gateways to personal development, we empower ourselves to face adversities head-on. We learn to view setbacks as stepping stones, failures as learning experiences, and hardships as catalysts for growth. Embracing challenges opens the doors to transformation, allowing us to cultivate the resilience, skills, and mindset necessary for success in all areas of life. So, let us embrace challenges and shift our perspectives, for within them lie the seeds of our greatness.

The Power of Consistency in Mental Training: Why regular mental conditioning is essential

In the realm of mental training, consistency is often hailed as the secret ingredient to unlocking one's true potential. While physical training is well-known for its emphasis on regularity, the importance of mental conditioning is often underrated and overshadowed. However, just as one can achieve physical prowess through consistent training, the same applies to mental fortitude and agility. In this chapter, we will explore the remarkable power of consistency in mental training and why it is absolutely essential for maximizing personal growth, focus, and overall well-being.

Understanding Mental Conditioning:

Before delving into the significance of consistency, let us first grasp the concept of mental conditioning. In simple terms, mental conditioning refers to the practice of strengthening and training the mind to achieve a desired state or outcome. It involves nurturing positive habits, developing resilience, and refining cognitive abilities. Mental conditioning can be likened to sculpting a masterpiece, where one shapes their thoughts, emotions, and reactions, ultimately shaping their reality.

The Fallacy of One-time Fixes:

The human mind is a complex entity influenced by various factors, including experiences, upbringing, and genetics. Often, individuals seek quick-fix solutions to overcome challenges or enhance their mental well-being. They may attend a single workshop, indulge in a random self-help book, or even practice meditation sporadically. However, expecting a significant transformation through isolated efforts is akin to believing that one can achieve physical fitness by exercising for a day or two.

The power of mental training lies not in its sporadic incorporation, but rather in its consistent integration into daily life. Just as physical exercise strengthens muscles over time, regular mental conditioning routines yield a more profound impact on cognitive abilities, emotional resilience, and overall mental health.

Building Habits and Reinforcing Neural Pathways:

Consistency in mental training allows individuals to establish positive habits and reinforce neural pathways that lead to optimal mental health and performance. Habits, as defined by renowned author Charles Duhigg, are "automatic behaviors triggered by contextual cues, like pulling out a cellphone upon hearing a notification." Consistent mental training helps create positive habits such as mindfulness, positive self-talk, and reframing negative thoughts. These habits, when ingrained in the mind through regular practice, become second nature.

On a neurological level, engaging in consistent mental conditioning strengthens the connection between neurons, ultimately shaping the way our brain processes information. The well-known adage, "neurons that fire together, wire together," illustrates how the repetition of mental exercises rewires our brain, allowing us to respond to challenges and opportunities with clarity and focus.

Maximizing Personal Growth:

Consistent mental conditioning is indispensable when it comes to personal growth. By incorporating regular practices into our daily routines, we foster a mindset of continuous improvement. Just as wanderers need a compass to navigate through unfamiliar territories, individuals seeking personal growth rely on consistency in mental training to guide their journey towards self-discovery and development.

Through regular introspection and self-reflection, one can identify their strengths, weaknesses, and areas for improvement. Consistent mental conditioning empowers individuals to set meaningful goals, develop strategies to achieve them, and maintain the motivation necessary to navigate the inevitable setbacks along the way.

Boosting Focus and Productivity:

In today's fast-paced world filled with distractions, maintaining focus has become an elusive skill. However, through consistent mental conditioning, individuals can reclaim control over their attention and enhance their productivity. Regular practice allows the mind to become more resistant to distractions, ensuring that it stays laser-focused on the task at hand.

Moreover, the cultivation of mindfulness, a key component of mental training, serves as an antidote to the constant mental chatter and anxieties that vie for attention. By training the mind to stay present in the current moment, individuals can optimize their mental resources, leading to heightened performance, efficiency, and overall effectiveness in various endeavors.

Enhancing Well-being:

Consistency in mental conditioning has a profound impact on overall well-being. In a world where stress, anxiety, and depression are pervasive, regular mental training offers a powerful defense mechanism. Through practices like meditation, gratitude, and self-care, individuals can strengthen their resilience, cultivate emotional balance, and reduce the detrimental effects of stress on both the mind and body.

Furthermore, consistent mental conditioning enables individuals to cultivate positive emotions and perspectives, fostering a sense of inner peace and contentment. By prioritizing their mental well-being and practicing self-compassion, individuals can lead healthier, more fulfilling lives.

The power of consistency in mental training cannot be overstated. Just as the physical body thrives on regular exercise, the mind blossoms with consistent mental conditioning. By embracing the practices outlined in this chapter and integrating them into our daily lives, we unlock the potential to achieve personal growth, sharpen focus, and enhance overall well-being.

Consistency is not a sprint; rather, it is a marathon that molds and shapes the mind over time. The journey towards mental fortitude requires dedication, discipline, and a commitment to change. As we embark on this path, let us remember that consistent mental conditioning is not merely a means to an end but a lifelong journey, enriching our lives in unimaginable ways.

Chapter 3: Overcoming Barriers to Mental Resilience

In the journey towards mental well-being, individuals encounter various obstacles and challenges that can hinder their progress. These barriers often arise from internal factors such as negative thinking patterns or external circumstances like societal pressures. Overcoming these barriers and cultivating mental resilience is essential for individuals to navigate through life's challenges successfully. This chapter will delve into several common barriers to mental resilience, explore their impact on individuals' well-being, and provide practical strategies to conquer these obstacles.

1. Limiting Beliefs:

One of the primary barriers to mental resilience lies in the limitations we place upon ourselves through our belief systems. These limiting beliefs can stem from childhood experiences, societal conditioning, or personal insecurities. For instance, a person who believes they are not smart enough may limit their academic pursuits or professional advancement. To overcome such limiting beliefs, it is crucial to identify and challenge them actively. By questioning the validity of these beliefs and replacing them with more empowering thoughts, individuals can unlock their potential and nurture mental resilience.

2. Negative Thinking Patterns:

Negative thinking patterns can significantly impact an individual's mental well-being and hinder their ability to bounce back from adversity. These patterns include catastrophizing, overgeneralization, and self-blame. For example, catastrophizing involves magnifying the significance of problems, which can lead to feelings of helplessness and anxiety. To overcome negative thinking patterns, individuals can practice cognitive reframing, which involves consciously replacing negative thoughts with positive or more realistic ones. Engaging in positive self-talk and seeking professional help, such as therapy or counseling, can also aid in breaking free from negative thinking patterns and building mental resilience.

3. Lack of Self-Compassion:

Forging resilience in the face of challenges requires self-compassion, yet many individuals struggle with being kind to themselves. They may hold themselves to unrealistic standards, engage in self-criticism, or struggle with feelings of unworthiness. Cultivating self-compassion involves treating oneself with kindness, understanding, and care, even in moments of difficulty or failure. Self-compassion enables individuals to bounce back from setbacks, learn from their mistakes, and maintain a positive outlook on life. Strategies to enhance self-compassion include practicing mindfulness, acknowledging one's emotions, and developing a supportive network of friends and loved ones.

4. Social Isolation:

Human beings thrive on connections and social interactions. However, social isolation has become increasingly prevalent in modern society, and it poses a significant barrier to mental resilience. Isolation can lead to feelings of loneliness, depression, and anxiety, and hinder individuals' ability to bounce back from adversity. Overcoming social isolation requires actively building and nurturing meaningful relationships. This can be achieved through joining social clubs, volunteering, or participating in community activities. Additionally, seeking support from friends, family, or mental health professionals can help individuals combat the negative effects of isolation and foster mental resilience.

5. External Pressures:

External pressures and societal expectations can often weigh individuals down and hamper their mental resilience. Examples include the pressure to conform, the unrealistic standards portrayed by media, or the need for constant achievement. Addressing these barriers involves challenging societal norms and defining one's own values and priorities. By setting realistic goals and focusing on personal growth rather than external validation, individuals can mitigate the impact of external pressures on their mental well-being and fortify their resilience.

6. Trauma and Adversity:

Experiencing trauma or significant adversity can pose immense challenges to an individual's mental resilience. Traumatic experiences can lead to feelings of fear, helplessness, and can impact one's overall outlook on life. Seeking professional help, such as therapy or counseling, is crucial in processing and healing from trauma. Engaging in self-care activities, practicing mindfulness, and utilizing coping strategies recommended by mental health professionals are also effective ways to overcome barriers and foster mental resilience in the face of trauma.

7. Lack of Adaptability:

Adapting to change and embracing uncertainty are vital components of mental resilience. However, many individuals struggle with letting go of control and resisting change. Cultivating adaptability involves developing a growth mindset—an attitude that sees challenges as opportunities for learning and growth. Engaging in activities that encourage flexibility, such as trying new hobbies or pursuing diverse experiences, can help individuals build their adaptability muscles and overcome this barrier to mental resilience.

Identifying Mental Roadblocks in Sports: Common mental challenges and how to spot them

In sports, the mind is just as crucial as physical ability. Along with proper training and physical preparedness, athletes must also possess a strong mental game to achieve their goals and excel in their chosen sport. However, various mental challenges can obstruct an athlete's progress and prevent them from reaching their full potential. This chapter aims to explore some common mental roadblocks in sports, shed light on how to identify them, and provide insights on overcoming these challenges.

1. Lack of Confidence:

Confidence is the cornerstone of success in sports. It fuels an athlete's belief in their abilities and allows them to perform optimally under pressure. However, many athletes struggle with low self-confidence, which can greatly hinder their performance. Signs of a lack of confidence may include self-doubt, negative self-talk, and a constant fear of failure.

Identifying Lack of Confidence:
- Frequent comparison to other athletes and a persistent feeling of insecurity.

- Displaying nervousness or anxiety before competitions.
- A constant need for reassurance and validation from coaches, teammates, or family members.
- Reluctance to take risks or avoid challenging situations.

Overcoming Lack of Confidence:

Building confidence requires consistent effort and a positive mindset. Athletes can employ various strategies to boost their confidence levels, such as:
- Setting achievable, short-term goals to reinforce a sense of accomplishment.
- Reflecting on past successes and acknowledging personal growth.
- Surrounding themselves with a support network of positive and encouraging individuals.
- Visualizing success and engaging in positive self-talk.

2. Performance Anxiety:

Performance anxiety, also known as stage fright, is a common mental roadblock that can afflict athletes of all levels. It often arises from an overwhelming fear of making mistakes, disappointing others, or performing poorly. This anxiety can severely impact an athlete's concentration, focus, and overall performance.

Identifying Performance Anxiety:
- Displaying pronounced nervousness or jitteriness before competitions.

- Difficulty sleeping or experiencing panic attacks leading up to important events.
- Obsessive thoughts about potential failures or negative outcomes.
- Inability to concentrate or worrying excessively during training or competition.

Overcoming Performance Anxiety:

Several strategies can help athletes overcome performance anxiety and perform at their best:
- Deep breathing exercises and relaxation techniques can help reduce anxiety levels.
- Developing pre-performance routines and rituals can provide comfort and familiarity.
- Visualizing success and mentally rehearsing successful performances can enhance confidence and alleviate anxiety.
- Utilizing positive affirmations and constructive self-talk to counteract negative thoughts.

3. Perfectionism:

While striving for excellence is commendable, perfectionism can become a significant mental roadblock for athletes. The relentless pursuit of flawlessness can hinder an athlete's progress, impact their mental health, and impede their overall performance. Perfectionists often set impossibly high standards and are overly critical of themselves.

Identifying Perfectionism:

- Excessive focus on minute details and a constant need for perfection.
- Becoming overly self-critical and displaying frustration or anger after minor mistakes.
- Failure to acknowledge personal achievements due to persistent feelings of inadequacy.
- Engaging in repetitive behaviors or rituals to achieve perceived perfection.

Overcoming Perfectionism:

Shifting away from perfectionism requires a recalibration of one's mindset and expectations. Athletes can adopt the following strategies to break free from the grip of perfectionism:
- Setting realistic and attainable goals that prioritize progress and development.
- Practicing self-compassion and embracing mistakes as opportunities for growth.
- Challenging negative thoughts and reframing them with positive and realistic perspectives.
- Seeking support from coaches, mentors, or sports psychologists to facilitate a healthier approach to performance.

4. Lack of Focus:

Maintaining focus is crucial for any athlete, as distractions can diminish performance and prevent the athlete from reaching their peak potential. A lack of focus can occur due to various reasons, such as external distractions, stress, or lack of mental preparedness.

Identifying Lack of Focus:

- Frequently experiencing mind-wandering or daydreaming during training or competitive situations.

- Failing to execute strategic plans or forgetting instructions.

- Easily getting distracted by crowd or environmental noises during competitions.

- Difficulty maintaining concentration for extended periods.

Overcoming Lack of Focus:

Enhancing focus requires dedication and practice. Athletes can implement the following techniques to improve their concentration and attention span:

- Utilizing mindfulness and meditation exercises to train the mind to stay present.

- Breaking down tasks or performances into smaller, manageable components to avoid feeling overwhelmed.

- Eliminating unnecessary distractions during training or competitions.

- Employing visualization techniques to enhance mental imagery and strengthen focus.

Strategies to Combat Negative Self-talk: Tools to transform one's internal dialogue

"Whether you think you can or you think you can't, you're right." These wise words from Henry Ford highlight the power of our thoughts and internal dialogue. Negative self-talk is an all-too-common phenomenon that can influence our emotions, actions, and mental well-being. It is crucial to identify and combat negative self-talk to cultivate a more positive and productive mindset. In this chapter, we will explore various strategies and tools that can help transform your internal dialogue, allowing you to take control of your thoughts and powerfully shape your reality.

Understanding Negative Self-talk:

Before diving into strategies to combat negative self-talk, it's vital to understand what it is and why it occurs. Negative self-talk refers to the inner voice and thoughts that habitually criticize, doubt, or belittle oneself. It often stems from past experiences, societal pressures, or self-perceived shortcomings. Negative self-talk can manifest in different ways, such as self-doubt, comparison to others, catastrophizing, and perfectionism.

1. Cultivate Self-awareness:

The first step in combating negative self-talk is cultivating self-awareness. Many negative thoughts occur automatically and unconsciously, making it challenging to recognize them. Start by paying close attention to your internal dialogue throughout the day. Whenever you catch yourself engaging in negative self-talk, pause and take note of the specific words, phrases, and feelings associated with those thoughts. This self-awareness will serve as the foundation for transformation.

2. Challenge Negative Thoughts:

Once you have identified negative self-talk patterns, the next step is to challenge them. Ask yourself if there is any evidence supporting these negative thoughts or if they are merely assumptions or distortions. Are there alternative explanations that are more positive or realistic? By questioning the validity of negative thoughts, you can begin to break their hold on your mind. Replace negative thoughts with affirmative statements that align with your goals and aspirations.

3. Practice Self-Compassion:

Self-compassion is a powerful tool in combating negative self-talk. Treat yourself with the same kindness and understanding you would offer a close friend going through a difficult time. Acknowledge that nobody is perfect, and it is okay to make mistakes or fall short of expectations. When negative thoughts arise, offer yourself words of encouragement and support. Remember that self-compassion fosters growth and resilience.

4. Reframe Limiting Beliefs:

Negative self-talk is often fueled by limiting beliefs, such as "I'm not good enough," or "I will never succeed." Challenge these beliefs by examining the evidence that supports or refutes them. Look for examples from your past where you have achieved success or overcome challenges. By reframing these limiting beliefs, you rewire your brain to focus on possibilities instead of limitations.

5. Surround Yourself with Positive Influences:

Your environment greatly impacts your internal dialogue. Surround yourself with positive role models, motivational books, podcasts, or supportive friends. Seek out mentors or individuals who have successfully transformed their own negative self-talk. Engage in activities that uplift and inspire you. The more positivity you expose yourself to, the more your own internal dialogue will reflect it.

6. Visualize Success:

Visualization is a powerful technique to combat negative self-talk. Take a few moments each day to mentally rehearse successful outcomes in your mind. Imagine yourself confidently speaking, achieving your goals, or overcoming obstacles. Engage all your senses and immerse yourself in the positive emotions attached to these visualizations. By repeatedly picturing success, you break the cycle of negative self-talk and reprogram your mind for achievement.

7. Practice Gratitude:

Gratitude has long been recognized as a potent antidote to negative thoughts. Make a habit of listing three things you are grateful for each day. Focus on the positive aspects of your life, no matter how small. By regularly acknowledging and appreciating the good in your life, you shift your mindset towards optimism and away from negative self-talk.

8. Embrace Failure and Learn from Mistakes:

Negative self-talk often intensifies after mistakes or failures. Embrace these setbacks as valuable learning opportunities instead of dwelling on self-criticism. Recognize that failures are part of the growth process and allow yourself to learn, adapt, and improve. By reframing failure, you diminish its power to trigger negative self-talk and instead leverage it for personal development.

9. Seek Support:

Recognize that transforming your internal dialogue is a journey that may require support from others. Seek out friends, family, or professionals who can provide guidance and encouragement. Share your struggles and goals with them, allowing them to hold you accountable and provide constructive feedback. Sometimes, an external perspective can illuminate blind spots and offer fresh insights to combat negative self-talk effectively.

10. Practice Mindfulness and Meditation:

Mindfulness and meditation are powerful tools to calm the mind and cultivate awareness of the present moment. By practicing mindfulness, you can observe negative thoughts without getting entangled in them. Meditation helps train the mind to focus on the breath, promoting a sense of calm and clarity. Regular mindfulness and meditation practice can reduce anxiety, increase self-awareness, and weaken the grip of negative self-talk.

Transforming negative self-talk is not an overnight process but a lifelong endeavor. By implementing these strategies and tools consistently, you can reshape your internal dialogue and develop a more positive and empowering mindset. Remember that self-growth and self-compassion are at the core of this transformation. Embrace the power of your thoughts and use them as a force to propel you towards success and fulfillment.

Emotional Regulation in High-Pressure Situations: Techniques to stay calm under pressure

In today's fast-paced and demanding world, high-pressure situations have become inevitable for many individuals. Whether it is facing a challenging deadline at work, delivering a crucial presentation, or competing in a high-stakes sports event, the ability to stay calm and maintain emotional regulation is essential. The way we handle these high-pressure scenarios can profoundly impact our success and well-being. This chapter explores various techniques that can help us navigate these situations effectively, enabling us to stay calm, focused, and perform at our best.

Understanding Emotional Regulation

Emotional regulation refers to the ability to manage and control our emotions when faced with challenging circumstances. It involves recognizing and acknowledging our emotions, understanding their triggers, and developing strategies to regulate them effectively. In high-pressure situations, emotional regulation becomes even more critical as stress, anxiety, and intense emotions can hinder our ability to think clearly and make sound decisions.

The Role of Self-Awareness

One of the fundamental aspects of emotional regulation is developing self-awareness. By understanding our emotions, we can gain insight into how they affect our behavior, thoughts, and overall performance. Taking a moment to reflect on our emotional state before and during high-pressure situations can provide valuable information about our triggers and how we typically respond.

Practicing Mindfulness

Mindfulness is a powerful technique that can significantly contribute to emotional regulation in high-pressure situations. By focusing our attention on the present moment without judgment, we can cultivate a sense of calmness and control. Mindfulness allows us to detach from negative thoughts and emotions, reducing their impact on our responses. Engaging in regular mindfulness exercises such as meditation or deep breathing can help build resilience and improve emotional regulation.

Managing Negative Self-Talk

Negative self-talk often exacerbates stress and anxiety in high-pressure situations. When faced with challenging circumstances, our inner voice may start to doubt our abilities, question our worthiness, or predict negative outcomes. To stay calm under pressure, it is crucial to identify and challenge this negative self-talk. Engaging in positive affirmations, reframing self-doubt into self-belief, and focusing on our strengths can help us maintain a confident and composed mindset.

Utilizing Cognitive Restructuring

Cognitive restructuring is a technique that involves examining and adjusting our thoughts and beliefs to promote a more positive and realistic perspective. During high-pressure situations, our minds can become overwhelmed with catastrophic thinking - imagining the worst-case scenarios and magnifying potential failures. By challenging these irrational thoughts and replacing them with more balanced and rational alternatives, we can reduce anxiety and maintain emotional stability.

Applying Stress Management Techniques

Stress is a common response to high-pressure situations and can significantly impact our emotional regulation. By implementing stress management techniques, we can effectively reduce stress levels and maintain a calm demeanor. Regular exercise, relaxation techniques such as deep breathing or progressive muscle relaxation, and engaging in hobbies or activities that bring joy and relaxation can all contribute to managing stress and improving emotional regulation.

Building Emotional Resilience

Emotional resilience plays a vital role in our ability to maintain composure and stay calm in high-pressure situations. Resilience allows us to bounce back from setbacks, adapt to changing circumstances, and maintain a positive mindset. Building emotional resilience involves developing a growth mindset, practicing self-compassion, seeking support from trusted individuals, and embracing failures as learning opportunities. By cultivating resilience, we can navigate high-pressure situations with confidence and grace.

Utilizing Visualization and Mental Imagery

Visualization and mental imagery techniques have been used for decades to enhance performance in various domains, including sports and public speaking. By vividly imagining ourselves succeeding in high-pressure situations, we can increase self-confidence, reduce anxiety, and improve emotional regulation. Carving out time to visualize positive outcomes and success can help us stay calm under pressure and perform at our best.

Implementing Time Management Strategies

In high-pressure situations, time constraints often add to the stress and can disrupt emotional regulation. Effective time management strategies can help alleviate this pressure and provide a sense of control. Breaking tasks into smaller, manageable chunks, prioritizing responsibilities, and setting realistic deadlines can help us stay calm and focused. Procrastination is often a significant stressor, so developing self-discipline and managing distractions become crucial in maintaining emotional well-being.

Seeking Support and Constructive Feedback

Seeking support from trusted individuals during high-pressure situations can provide not only emotional reassurance but also valuable insights and guidance. Confiding in someone who understands the situation can alleviate stress and help put things into perspective. Additionally, seeking constructive feedback from mentors or coaches can offer valuable advice and help improve performance, enhancing emotional regulation in subsequent high-pressure scenarios.

Emotional regulation is a vital skill to navigate high-pressure situations effectively. By developing self-awareness, practicing mindfulness, managing negative self-talk, utilizing cognitive restructuring, applying stress management techniques, building emotional resilience, utilizing visualization and mental imagery, implementing time management strategies, and seeking support and feedback, we can build our capacity to stay calm and composed when the pressure is at its peak.

Ultimately, mastering emotional regulation in high-pressure situations is a process that requires consistent practice and self-reflection. By adopting these techniques and making them a part of our daily lives, we can develop emotional resilience and thrive in the face of adversity. Remember, staying calm under pressure is not just a sign of strength; it is a skill that can maximize our potential and lead to success in both personal and professional endeavors.

The Threat of Burnout in Young Athletes: Recognizing signs and preventing athlete burnout

In today's highly competitive sports landscape, young athletes often face intense pressure to succeed. While this level of dedication can be beneficial for their development, it can also lead to burnout – a serious concern that can have long-lasting consequences. This chapter aims to delve into the topic of burnout in young athletes, exploring its definition, potential causes, signs to recognize, and most importantly, strategies for prevention.

Understanding Burnout:

Burnout is a state of emotional, physical, and mental exhaustion caused by excessive and prolonged stress. While burnout can affect people of all ages, it is especially prevalent among young athletes who juggle multiple commitments and face intense expectations from coaches, parents, and even themselves. When left unaddressed, burnout can have a detrimental impact on the overall well-being, performance, and future participation of these young athletes.

Causes of Athlete Burnout:

Several factors contribute to the development of burnout in young athletes. Firstly, the pressure to succeed and meet high expectations set by coaches, parents, and even self-imposed can be overwhelming. Young athletes may feel compelled to excel in various areas, such as school, training, competitions, and social life, leading to non-stop demands on their time and energy.

Moreover, the lack of control over their own sporting journey can contribute to burnout. If young athletes feel like they have little say in their training schedules, competition participation, or even choice of sport, they may become disenchanted and lose motivation over time.

Additionally, the absence of proper support systems plays a critical role in the development of burnout. When young athletes lack a strong support network, including coaches, parents, teammates, and friends who understand and empathize with their challenges, they can feel isolated and overwhelmed, further exacerbating burnout.

Recognizing the Signs of Burnout:

To effectively address and prevent burnout in young athletes, it is crucial to recognize potential warning signs. While each individual may exhibit different symptoms, some commonly observed signs of burnout include:

1. Frequent physical and emotional exhaustion: Young athletes may experience persistent tiredness, reduced energy levels, sleep

disturbances, and an overall feeling of being physically and mentally drained.

2. Decline in performance: Burnout can lead to a decline in performance as young athletes lose their motivation, focus, and drive to excel in their sport. They may display inconsistent performance, reduced effort, or lack of enjoyment during training and competition.

3. Emotional and psychological changes: Young athletes may exhibit mood swings, irritability, increased anxiety, decreased self-confidence, and feelings of detachment from their sport. They may also become more susceptible to depression and experience a loss of pleasure in activities they once enjoyed.

4. Frequent injuries and illnesses: Burnout weakens the immune system, making young athletes more prone to injuries, persistent fatigue, and susceptibility to illnesses. These physical setbacks can further contribute to their mental and emotional exhaustion.

5. Social withdrawal: When experiencing burnout, young athletes may withdraw from their social interactions with teammates, friends, and even family members. They may isolate themselves and lose interest in maintaining relationships, finding solace in solitude instead.

Preventing and Addressing Burnout:

To combat the threat of burnout in young athletes, it is imperative to implement preventive strategies and create a supportive environment. Here are some effective measures to consider:

1. Promote open communication: Coaches, parents, and athletes should encourage honest and open conversations about stress, expectations, and any concerns related to burnout. By fostering a safe and non-judgmental environment, athletes will feel comfortable discussing their challenges and seeking support when needed.

2. Foster athlete autonomy: Empowering young athletes to have more control over their training, competition schedules, and decision-making processes can significantly reduce the risk of burnout. This autonomy allows athletes to take ownership of their sporting journey, promoting a sense of purpose and motivation.

3. Encourage multi-sport participation: Engaging in a variety of sports and physical activities can prevent burnout by reducing the repetitive demands and pressure associated with specialization in a single sport. Multi-sport participation also enhances overall athletic development and encourages a more balanced approach to sports.

4. Establish proper recovery periods: Incorporating adequate rest and recovery days in training programs is essential to prevent burnout. Young athletes should have periods of downtime to relax, recover, and pursue activities unrelated to their primary sport.

5. Cultivate a supportive network: Parents, coaches, and teammates should strive to create a supportive and positive environment for young athletes. By demonstrating care, empathy, and understanding, this network can help alleviate stress, boost resilience, and prevent burnout.

Recognizing and addressing the threat of burnout in young athletes is essential for their long-term physical, mental, and emotional well-being. By understanding the causes, recognizing the signs, and implementing preventive strategies, coaches, parents, and athletes can work together to ensure a healthier and more sustainable sporting experience. Ultimately, it is crucial to foster an environment where young athletes can thrive, grow, and continue enjoying their chosen sport for years to come.

Chapter 4: Developing a Growth Mindset

In this chapter, we will dive into the concept of developing a growth mindset and explore how it can positively impact our lives. A growth mindset is about believing in the potential for growth and improvement, rather than clinging to fixed beliefs about our abilities and limitations. It is an essential trait that can enable us to find success, overcome challenges, and cultivate resilience. By embracing a growth mindset, we unlock the power to achieve our goals and realize our full potential.

Discovering the Power of Mindset

Have you ever wondered why some people seem to effortlessly achieve their goals, while others constantly struggle? The answer often lies in their mindset – the underlying beliefs and attitudes they have about intelligence, abilities, and success. Renowned psychologist Carol Dweck introduced the idea of fixed and growth mindsets in her groundbreaking research. According to Dweck, individuals with a fixed mindset believe that intelligence and talent are fixed traits that cannot be changed, while those with a growth mindset understand that abilities can be developed through hard work, dedication, and learning.

Understanding Fixed Mindset

Individuals with a fixed mindset tend to view their abilities as fixed and limited. They believe that success is based on inherent talent rather than effort. When faced with challenges or setbacks, those with a fixed mindset often become discouraged and give up easily. They perceive failure as a sign of incompetence and are afraid to take risks. As a result, they may avoid challenging tasks and miss out on valuable learning opportunities. This fixed mindset can act as a roadblock to personal and professional growth.

Cultivating a Growth Mindset

Thankfully, a mindset is not set in stone, and it is entirely possible to cultivate a growth mindset with dedication and practice. Embracing a growth mindset entails recognizing that our abilities are not fixed, but can be developed over time. Here are some strategies to help you develop a growth mindset:

1. Embrace Challenges

Instead of shying away from challenges, seek them out. Challenges provide valuable learning opportunities and allow you to stretch beyond your comfort zone. Embracing challenges fosters growth, as it forces you to develop new skills and push your boundaries. Remember, the most significant growth occurs outside your comfort zone.

2. Emphasize Effort

Rather than focusing solely on outcomes or results, shift your attention to the effort you put into your endeavors. Recognize that hard work and persistence are the keys to growth and success. By appreciating the process and the effort required, you will become more resilient and better equipped to handle setbacks and obstacles.

3. Embrace Failure as a Teacher

Instead of viewing failure as a reflection of your abilities, reframe it as an opportunity for growth. Understand that failure is an inherent part of the learning process and essential for improvement. Embrace failure as a teacher, analyzing what went wrong and identifying areas for growth. By adopting this mindset, you will approach challenges with more resilience and determination.

4. Cultivate a Love for Learning

A growth mindset is rooted in a love for learning. Embrace curiosity and a thirst for knowledge. Seek out opportunities to learn and grow, whether through formal education, reading, or other experiences. By adopting a lifelong learner mindset, you will continuously develop new skills and expand your intellectual horizons.

5. Shift from Seeking Approval to Seeking Improvement

Many individuals with a fixed mindset seek external validation and approval. Instead of relying on others' opinions, shift your focus to seeking constant self-improvement. Understand that your journey is unique, and comparing yourself to others only limits your growth potential. Embrace your own progress and strive to become a better version of yourself.

6. Surround Yourself with Growth-Oriented Individuals

The people we surround ourselves with have a significant impact on our mindset. Surround yourself with individuals who believe in growth and inspire you to pursue your goals. Engage in discussions, collaborate on projects, and seek support from like-minded individuals who are constantly striving for personal growth. Developing a growth mindset is an essential component of personal and professional growth. By adopting a growth mindset, we can overcome obstacles, achieve our goals, and unlock our true potential. Remember, a growth mindset is not something we are born with but can be developed through consistent effort and practice. Embrace challenges, emphasize effort, and reframe failure as an opportunity for growth. Cultivate a love for learning, shift your focus from seeking approval to seeking improvement, and surround yourself with growth-oriented individuals. By adopting these strategies and nurturing a growth mindset, you can transform your life and create a future filled with possibilities.

The Principles of a Growth Mindset: Introduction to Carol Dweck's groundbreaking concept

The human mind is an intriguing phenomenon, capable of incredible achievements and personal growth. It has long been a subject of great interest for psychologists, philosophers, and educators. How can we tap into our potential, overcome challenges, and achieve our goals? Is there a key to unlocking our true capabilities? These questions have driven many scholars to explore the various aspects of the human mind, leading to fascinating insights and groundbreaking concepts.

One such concept that has had an indelible impact on the field of psychology and education is the growth mindset. Developed by renowned psychologist Carol S. Dweck, the growth mindset proposes that our beliefs about our abilities and intelligence significantly influence our achievement and success. In this chapter, we will delve into the principles of a growth mindset, exploring the core ideas that underpin this transformative concept.

Understanding Mindsets

To comprehend the concept of a growth mindset, it is essential to first understand the notion of mindsets itself. Mindsets are deeply ingrained beliefs about ourselves, our abilities, and the world around us. These beliefs shape our perception, behavior, and responses to challenges, thereby influencing our overall personal growth. Dweck identifies two primary mindsets: the growth mindset and the fixed mindset.

The fixed mindset is characterized by the belief that intelligence and abilities are fixed traits; we are born with a certain level of intelligence, and there is little room for improvement. Those with a fixed mindset tend to view failure as a reflection of their inherent limitations, often avoiding challenges for fear of exposing their inadequacies. They perceive effort as fruitless, considering ability to be predetermined and unchangeable.

In contrast, individuals with a growth mindset view intelligence and abilities as malleable qualities that can be developed through dedication, effort, and perseverance. They embrace challenges, view failure as an opportunity to learn and grow, and understand that hard work can lead to improvement. People with a growth mindset thrive on challenges and are driven by a desire to continually better themselves.

The Power of Beliefs

At the heart of the growth mindset lies the power of our beliefs. According to Dweck, our mindset strongly influences how we approach and navigate our lives. Our beliefs about intelligence and abilities shape not only our attitude towards learning but also impact our self-perception, motivation, resilience, and ultimate achievement.

Individuals with a growth mindset hold the belief that effort is the pathway to mastery. They recognize that abilities can be developed and enhanced through deliberate practice, and setbacks or failures are stepping stones towards improvement. Consequently, they embrace challenges, eagerly seek feedback, and persist in the face of adversity.

Conversely, those with a fixed mindset tend to view effort as a futile endeavor. Believing that intelligence and abilities are predetermined, individuals with a fixed mindset often shy away from challenges to protect their self-image. They are more likely to be discouraged by setbacks and failures, often questioning their worth and ability.

Cultivating a Growth Mindset

While the concept of a growth mindset may seem rather straightforward, developing and nurturing it is a journey that requires active effort and self-awareness. It involves challenging our existing beliefs, reframing our perspective on failure, and adopting strategies that promote growth and development. Here are some key principles that can help cultivate a growth mindset:

1. Embrace Challenges: Embracing challenges is an integral part of developing a growth mindset. Challenges provide opportunities for

learning and growth, allowing us to expand our abilities and gain new insights. By willingly stepping out of our comfort zones, we open ourselves up to new possibilities and cultivate a mindset that thrives on continuous improvement.

2. Embrace the Power of "YET": Instead of perceiving failure as evidence of our limitations, adopt a mindset that acknowledges the power of the word "yet." When faced with setbacks, remind yourself that you haven't achieved your goals "yet." This simple shift in language can create a sense of possibility and motivate you to persist in your efforts towards growth and mastery.

3. Embrace Effort: Effort is key to unlocking our potential and nurturing a growth mindset. Recognize that sustained effort, deliberate practice, and consistent learning are the building blocks of success. Celebrate hard work and dedication, understanding that true mastery is not achieved overnight, but through a continuous commitment to growth.

4. Embrace Feedback and Criticism: Feedback, even when critical, is valuable for growth. Embrace feedback as a means to learn and improve, rather than as a personal attack. Understand that feedback is an opportunity to discover new insights, refine your skills, and propel yourself towards greater success.

Applying the Growth Mindset in Education

The growth mindset has significant implications for education and has the potential to revolutionize the way we approach teaching and learning. By creating an environment that promotes a growth mindset, educators can empower students, boost their motivation, and foster a love for learning.

In a growth-oriented classroom, students are encouraged to take risks, explore new ideas, and embrace challenges. Mistakes and failures are seen as opportunities for growth and learning, rather than as indicators of incompetence. Teachers emphasize the process of learning rather than just the end result, nurturing students' intellectual curiosity and promoting a love for knowledge.

The principles of a growth mindset, as expounded by Carol S. Dweck, offer profound insights into our potential for growth and personal development. By recognizing the power of our beliefs, embracing challenges, and valuing effort, we can cultivate a mindset that fosters resilience, motivation, and a thirst for knowledge.

In the subsequent chapters, we will delve deeper into the practical application of the growth mindset in various domains of life, from personal relationships to professional endeavors. By understanding and harnessing the principles of a growth mindset, we can unlock our true potential and embark on a journey of continuous growth and fulfillment.

The Athlete's Journey from Fixed to Growth Mindset: Steps to transition between the two mindsets

In the realm of sports, the mindset of an athlete plays a critical role in determining their success. Athletes who possess a growth mindset, believing that their abilities can be developed through hard work, dedication, and perseverance, often outperform those with a fixed mindset, who believe their talents and abilities are fixed traits. Transitioning from a fixed to a growth mindset is a transformative journey that requires conscious effort and deliberate practice. In this chapter, we will explore the steps an athlete can take to transition between these two mindsets and unlock their true potential on the field, court, or track.

Understanding the Fixed Mindset:

The fixed mindset is based on the belief that abilities are innate and unchangeable. Athletes with a fixed mindset often see their failures as a reflection of their personal limitations or lack of talent. They may perceive setbacks as signs that they are not good enough, leading to a fear of failure and a desire to stick to what they know they are good at rather than taking risks.

Step 1: Self-awareness and Acceptance

The first step in transitioning from a fixed to a growth mindset is self-awareness. Athletes must recognize and accept that they have been operating from a fixed mindset and acknowledge the impact it has had on their performance. This self-reflection helps athletes to take ownership of their mindset and opens the door for growth and change.

Step 2: Embrace Challenges and Failure

To adopt a growth mindset, athletes must embrace challenges and reframe failure as a learning opportunity. The fear of failure often holds athletes back, preventing them from venturing outside their comfort zone. By recognizing that failure is an integral part of growth and improvement, athletes can start viewing challenges as stepping stones towards success rather than insurmountable obstacles.

Step 3: Cultivate a Learning Orientation

Transitioning to a growth mindset requires a shift in focus from outcomes to the process of learning and improvement. Athletes must develop a genuine passion for learning and seek opportunities to expand their knowledge and skills. They should approach every training session, competition, or practice with a thirst for acquiring new information and understanding.

Step 4: Effort and Hard work

In a growth mindset, athletes value effort and hard work over talent alone. They understand that talent may provide a head start, but it is consistent effort and deliberate practice that leads to mastery. Athletes must be willing to put in the necessary time and effort, even when faced with setbacks or challenges. They should approach every practice session with dedication and focus, understanding that growth comes from pushing beyond their limits.

Step 5: Adopt a Positive Mindset

A key element in transitioning to a growth mindset is adopting a positive attitude. Athletes should reframe their self-talk and replace negative thoughts with positive affirmations. By recognizing and challenging their negative beliefs, athletes can create a positive environment that nurtures growth and fosters resilience.

Step 6: Seek Feedback and Support

Athletes on the journey towards a growth mindset should actively seek feedback from coaches, teammates, and mentors. This feedback helps identify areas for improvement and provides guidance on how to develop specific skills. Athletes should also surround themselves with a supportive network of individuals who believe in their potential and encourage their growth.

Step 7: Embrace the Process

Transitioning from a fixed to a growth mindset is not an overnight transformation. It requires patience, perseverance, and an understanding that growth takes time. Athletes must learn to appreciate the small wins and milestones along the way, celebrating progress rather than solely focusing on the end result.

Step 8: Maintain a Growth Mindset

Finally, it is essential for athletes to continuously nurture and maintain their growth mindset. This can be achieved through consistent practice, self-reflection, and staying motivated. Athletes should remind themselves regularly of the progress they have made and set new goals that challenge them to reach even greater heights.

Transitioning from a fixed to a growth mindset is a journey that offers athletes the opportunity to tap into their full potential. By following the steps outlined in this chapter, athletes can shift their mindset, liberating themselves from self-imposed limitations and embracing the process of growth and improvement. Embracing challenges, cultivating a learning orientation, valuing effort, adopting a positive mindset, seeking feedback, and maintaining consistency are crucial elements in this transformative journey. With a growth mindset, athletes can overcome obstacles, achieve greatness, and leave a lasting legacy in their chosen sport.

Embracing Failures as Learning Experiences: Changing the narrative on setbacks in sports

In the world of sports, setbacks and failures are inevitable. Whether you're an amateur player or a professional athlete, you will undoubtedly face moments of disappointment, defeat, and setbacks throughout your career. However, the way we perceive and respond to these setbacks can have a profound impact on our growth, both as athletes and as individuals. In this chapter, we will explore the concept of embracing failures as learning experiences, and the tremendous power it holds in transforming our mindset and approach to sports.

The Stigma of Failure

Failure is often stigmatized in society, and sports are no exception. Athletes are often judged solely based on their wins, losses, and their ability to perform under pressure. However, this narrow-minded focus on results alone fails to acknowledge the invaluable lessons that setbacks can teach us. Instead of viewing failures as indicators of inadequacy or insurmountable obstacles, embracing them as learning experiences can help us reframe our mindset and redirect our efforts towards growth and improvement.

The Growth Mindset

A key component of embracing failures as learning experiences lies in adopting a growth mindset. Developed by renowned psychologist Carol Dweck, the growth mindset is a belief that our abilities and intelligence can be developed through dedication, hard work, and learning from our mistakes. Athletes who possess a growth mindset see failures as opportunities for growth and improvement, rather than as setbacks or indicators of their talent.

When athletes embrace a growth mindset, they no longer view failures as permanent and demoralizing. Instead, they perceive setbacks as temporary hurdles that can be overcome with perseverance, effort, and the willingness to learn from their mistakes. This shift in mindset allows athletes to bounce back stronger, more resilient, and armed with a vast array of lessons and experiences that will undoubtedly benefit them in the long run.

Redefining Success

Another crucial aspect of embracing failures as learning experiences is redefining the notion of success. Traditional definitions of success in sports often revolve around winning, achieving personal bests, or securing a spot on a prestigious team. However, when we limit success solely to these outcomes, we disregard the journey, the effort invested, and the growth that occurs along the way.

By reframing success as a holistic measure of growth, resilience, and the ability to bounce back from failures, athletes can liberate themselves from the constant pressure to achieve specific outcomes. Instead of fixating on results, they learn to appreciate the process, the incremental improvements, and the valuable insights gained from failures. This shift in perspective fosters a healthier approach to sports, where the focus lies not solely on winning, but on personal growth, self-improvement, and the joy of the game.

Learning from Failures

Failure, when embraced and analyzed, offers an unparalleled opportunity for learning and self-improvement. When athletes encounter setbacks, they have a chance to reflect on what went wrong, identify their weaknesses, and develop strategies to address them. Whether it's a missed shot, a costly mistake, or a defeat, failures provide valuable feedback that can guide future training, refine technique, and shape future performances.

Athletes who embrace failures as learning experiences actively seek feedback from coaches, teammates, and even opponents. They are open to constructive criticism, acknowledging that it is through recognizing and understanding their flaws that they can transform their weaknesses into strengths. Moreover, they recognize that it is in the face of adversity that true character and resilience are forged, creating an unyielding mindset that propels them forward.

Cultivating a Supportive Environment

To truly embrace failures as learning experiences, athletes require a supportive environment that encourages risk-taking, vulnerability, and personal growth. Coaches, teammates, and even fans play a pivotal role in shaping this environment by fostering an inclusive and positive culture, free from judgment or retribution for mistakes. Coaches, in particular, can make an enormous impact by reframing failures as opportunities for growth, demonstrating empathy and understanding, and providing constructive feedback. By cultivating an environment that normalizes failures and reframes them as vital steps in the journey towards excellence, athletes will feel more comfortable taking risks, pushing their boundaries, and embracing the inevitable setbacks that come with the territory.

Embracing failures as learning experiences is a transformative concept that has the power to redefine the narrative on setbacks in sports. By adopting a growth mindset, redefining success, and viewing failures as opportunities for growth and improvement, athletes can tap into their true potential and unlock unimaginable levels of resilience, determination, and self-improvement.

No longer will failures be seen as crippling defeats, but rather as stepping stones towards greatness. In this chapter, we have explored the importance of a growth mindset, redefining success, learning from failures, and cultivating a supportive environment. It is through embracing setbacks as valuable learning experiences that athletes can truly harness their full potential and become not only exceptional athletes but remarkable individuals.

Cultivating a Curious Mind in Training: How constant learning can fuel mental growth

In our fast-paced and ever-evolving world, the ability to cultivate a curious mind has never been more crucial. With technology advancing at lightning speed and information available at our fingertips, being able to adapt, learn, and grow has become essential. This chapter explores the profound impact of constant learning on mental growth and offers strategies to cultivate curiosity throughout our lives, with a particular focus on training and development.

The Power of Curiosity

Curiosity, often described as the thirst for knowledge, is a fundamental human trait that drives exploration, discovery, and innovation. From an early age, we begin to ask questions, seeking to understand the world around us. This innate curiosity contributes significantly to our learning and cognitive development. However, as we transition into adulthood, we often lose touch with this natural inquisitiveness, settling into routines and complacency.

Constant learning reignites the flame of curiosity within us, allowing us to embrace new perspectives, challenge assumptions, and develop a growth mindset. It provides a mental workout, stimulating the brain and fostering neural connections. The more we learn, the more our capacity to learn expands, setting off a virtuous cycle of knowledge acquisition and mental growth.

Cultivating Curiosity in Training and Development

Training and development provide fertile ground for cultivating a curious mind. Whether it be professional workshops, educational courses, or personal development programs, these opportunities serve as catalysts for continuous learning. Here, we explore several strategies to infuse the spirit of curiosity into training and development initiatives:

1. Embrace the Art of Questioning

Incorporating questioning techniques into training sessions encourages participants to explore, analyze, and critically think about the subject matter. Facilitators should adopt open-ended questions that promote discussion and debate, encouraging learners to challenge existing knowledge and seek alternative perspectives. By embracing the art of questioning, participants are propelled into an intellectual inquiry that fosters their curiosity and expands their mental landscape.

2. Nurture a Safe Learning Environment

A safe and non-judgmental learning environment is essential for cultivating curiosity. When individuals feel valued, respected, and free to express their thoughts, they are more likely to step out of their comfort zones and embrace new ideas. Creating an atmosphere of psychological safety allows learners to explore diverse concepts, take risks, and learn from their mistakes. By removing the fear of failure, curiosity flourishes, and mental growth becomes inevitable.

3. Incorporate Real-World Applications

Training and development programs often require individuals to learn new concepts or skills. By connecting these teachings to real-world applications, trainers can enhance participants' curiosity. Showcasing examples from different fields, inspiring success stories, and demonstrating how the newly acquired knowledge can be practically applied, stimulates curiosity by highlighting the potential impact of learning on personal and professional growth.

4. Encourage Multidisciplinary Learning

Encouraging learners to step outside their comfort zones and explore diverse topics can ignite their curiosity. Multidisciplinary learning allows individuals to gain insights from various fields, drawing connections, and fostering a holistic perspective. By encouraging participants to explore beyond their core areas of expertise, trainers create an environment where curiosity thrives, leading to mental growth through the synthesis of knowledge.

5. Provide Autonomy and Flexibility

To fuel curiosity in training and development, it is essential to provide learners with autonomy and flexibility. Allowing individuals to explore topics of personal interest within the broader framework of the program encourages intrinsic motivation and deep engagement. By tailoring their learning journey, participants take ownership of their growth, fostering their sense of curiosity and maximizing their mental development.

6. Foster Collaborative Learning

Collaborative learning experiences can be highly effective in cultivating curiosity. By encouraging participants to collaborate, exchange ideas, and challenge each other's perspectives, trainers create an environment that stimulates curiosity. Collaborative learning promotes active engagement, invites diverse viewpoints, and encourages learners to question assumptions, ultimately fueling their mental growth.

Sustaining Curiosity Beyond Training

While training and development programs provide an ideal environment for nurturing curiosity, it is essential to sustain this mindset beyond the confines of structured learning. Here are a few strategies to continue cultivating a curious mind in our everyday lives:

1. Create a Curiosity Journal

Maintaining a curiosity journal can be a powerful tool for continuing the learning journey. Whether through writing, sketching, or capturing ideas digitally, regularly reflecting on our experiences, discoveries, and questions strengthens our curiosity muscle. By actively seeking new knowledge and making it a habit to document our insights, we foster a continuous learning mindset that supports ongoing mental growth.

2. Seek Novel Experiences

Breaking free from monotonous routines and seeking novel experiences is key to sustaining curiosity. Exploring different cultures, trying new hobbies, or engaging in activities outside our comfort zones widens our horizons and keeps our minds engaged. The pursuit of novelty not only fosters intellectual growth but also enhances our overall well-being. By embracing new experiences, we embrace the unknown and ignite our curiosity further.

3. Foster a Growth Mindset

Holding a growth mindset is vital for maintaining a curious mind. Embracing the belief that our abilities and intelligence can be developed with effort and practice allows us to approach challenges as opportunities for growth. By reframing failures as learning experiences and persisting in the face of adversity, we nurture our curiosity, continuously seeking new avenues for growth and mental development.

Cultivating a curious mind through constant learning is essential for our mental growth in an ever-changing world. By embracing the art of questioning, fostering a safe learning environment, connecting knowledge to real-world applications, encouraging multidisciplinary learning, providing autonomy and flexibility, and promoting collaborative learning, we can infuse curiosity into our training and development initiatives. By sustaining curiosity beyond structured learning through curiosity journals, seeking novel experiences, and cultivating a growth mindset, we ensure lifelong mental growth. Embracing constant learning as a way of life, we become architects of our mental development, continually expanding our horizons and embracing new opportunities for growth and innovation.

Chapter 5: Techniques to Bolster Mental Toughness

In our journey towards achieving our goals, developing mental toughness plays a crucial role. The ability to overcome challenges, persevere in the face of obstacles, and stay focused on our objectives is what separates successful individuals from the rest. In this chapter, we will delve into various techniques that can bolster mental toughness and help us unlock our true potential. By applying these strategies consistently, we can enhance our mental strength and resilience, paving the way for a more fulfilling and successful life.

1. Reframe Negative Thoughts:

One of the first steps to building mental toughness is learning to reframe negative thoughts. Our minds can often be our worst enemy, creating doubts and fears that hold us back. By reframing negative beliefs into positive ones, we can harness the power of optimism and resilience.

For instance, if you find yourself thinking, "I'll never be able to complete this project on time," reframe it as, "I have overcome challenges before, and I am capable of handling this one as well." By consciously challenging and replacing negative thoughts with positive affirmations, we can strengthen our mental fortitude.

2. Set Realistic Goals:

Goal setting is an essential aspect of mental toughness. However, it is crucial to set realistic goals that are within our control and align with our capabilities. Unrealistic expectations can lead to disappointment and a decrease in confidence. By setting achievable milestones, we can maintain a sense of progress and motivation along our journey.

Furthermore, breaking larger goals into smaller, manageable tasks allows us to celebrate small victories and maintain our momentum. This approach helps us build mental resilience by fostering a sense of accomplishment and reminding us of our ability to overcome challenges.

3. Develop a Growth Mindset:

Having a growth mindset is fundamental to developing mental toughness. It is the belief that our abilities and intelligence can be developed through dedication and hard work. Embracing challenges, seeing failures as learning opportunities, and persisting in the face of setbacks are key traits of a growth mindset.

By shifting our perspective to view challenges as stepping stones rather than stumbling blocks, we can cultivate mental resilience. Remember, failures are not indictments of our abilities, but rather opportunities for growth and improvement.

4. Practice Mindfulness and Emotional Regulation:

In the pursuit of mental toughness, it is essential to foster mindfulness and emotional regulation. Mindfulness involves being fully present in the moment, aware of our thoughts and emotions without judgment. This practice allows us to develop a deeper understanding of ourselves and our triggers, leading to better emotional regulation.

When faced with challenging situations, take a moment to breathe and observe your emotions without being fully consumed by them. Practice techniques such as meditation, deep breathing exercises, and journaling to gain control over your emotional state. By mastering our emotions, we can stay calm, composed, and focused, even in the most stressful circumstances.

5. Cultivate a Supportive Network:

Having a strong support system is invaluable when it comes to mental toughness. Surrounding ourselves with like-minded individuals who believe in our capabilities and support our dreams can provide the motivation and encouragement we need during difficult times.

Seek out mentors, coaches, or friends who have faced similar challenges and come out victorious. Their insights and guidance will prove invaluable on our journey to mental toughness. By fostering positive relationships, we not only gain support but also develop our leadership skills and learn from the experiences of others.

6. Embrace Discomfort and Growth:

To truly bolster our mental toughness, we must embrace discomfort and willingly step outside our comfort zones. Growth only occurs when we push our boundaries and challenge ourselves. By intentionally seeking out new experiences and taking calculated risks, we expand our capabilities and develop resilience in the face of adversity.

Remember, it is in discomfort that we find growth. So, take on new challenges, try new approaches, and continuously push yourself beyond what feels safe or familiar. The more comfortable you become with discomfort, the more mentally tough you will become.

7. Practice Visualization and Positive Self-Talk:

Visualization and positive self-talk are powerful tools to strengthen mental toughness. By engaging in vivid imagery of achieving our goals, we stimulate our subconscious mind, heightening our motivation and belief in our abilities.

Incorporate positive self-talk into your daily routine by using affirmations and mantras that reinforce your confidence. Repeat statements such as, "I have what it takes to succeed," or "I am resilient and capable of overcoming any obstacle." By consistently reinforcing positive beliefs about ourselves, we strengthen our mental resilience and fortitude.

Developing mental toughness is a lifelong process, and it requires dedication, practice, and commitment. By incorporating these techniques into our daily lives, we can cultivate a resilient mindset that propels us towards success. Remember, mental toughness is not about eliminating difficulties; it is about building the capacity to overcome them. Through reframing negative thoughts, goal setting, embracing discomfort, and nurturing supportive relationships, we can unlock our true potential and achieve the life we desire. So, begin your journey to mental toughness today - invest in your mindset, and the possibilities are limitless.

The Power of Visualization in Sports: Using imagery to prepare the mind for competition

In the realm of sports, athletes often rely on their physical abilities and technical skills to excel in their respective disciplines. However, what separates the exceptional athletes from the rest is their ability to master the mental aspects of their sport. One such powerful tool that has gained immense popularity is visualization or imagery. This chapter delves into the profound impact of visualization in sports, exploring how athletes can utilize this technique to prepare their minds for competition and enhance their overall performance. By integrating imagery into their training regimens, athletes can unlock hidden potential, improve focus, boost confidence, and overcome mental barriers that hinder their success.

Understanding Visualization in Sports

Visualization, also known as mental imagery or mental rehearsal, involves creating vivid mental pictures or simulations in the mind to rehearse particular sporting actions or scenarios. It encompasses not just visual imagery, but also incorporates other senses such as auditory, kinesthetic, and emotional components, enabling athletes to immerse themselves fully in the imagined experience. By utilizing this powerful tool, athletes can simulate and familiarize themselves with complex movements and situations, ultimately enhancing their performance when facing similar challenges in real competitions.

Preparing the Mind for Competition

One of the fundamental benefits of visualization is its ability to prepare the mind for competition. Athletes spend a significant amount of time training their bodies, but often neglect to train their minds with the same intensity. Visualization provides athletes with a unique opportunity to mentally rehearse and prepare for the demands of their sport, ensuring that they are mentally and emotionally ready when they step onto the field, court, or track.

Visualization can be utilized in varying forms to aid in this preparation. Athletes can imagine themselves executing flawless techniques, picturing the exact sequences of movements required for their sport. By repeatedly practicing these mental simulations, athletes establish a neural pathway in their brains, making it easier to reproduce the desired actions during actual competitions.

Enhancing Focus and Concentration

Another significant advantage of visualization is its ability to enhance focus and concentration. In the fast-paced world of sports, maintaining unwavering concentration is crucial for peak performance. However, distractions and external factors can easily disrupt an athlete's focus. Visualization allows athletes to eliminate external distractions by creating an internal environment in which they are fully engrossed in their imagined scenario.

Through visualization, athletes can keep their minds centered on the task at hand, shutting out any interference that may arise during competition. By rehearsing mental images of themselves performing flawlessly, athletes build self-confidence and improve concentration, allowing them to execute their skills with laser-like precision when it matters most.

Boosting Confidence and Motivation

Confidence plays a pivotal role in an athlete's success. It is often said that the most formidable opponents an athlete will face can be found within their own mind. Self-doubt and negative thoughts can severely hinder performance. Visualization serves as a potent tool to combat these mental barriers and boost an athlete's confidence.

By vividly picturing successful performances, athletes create a positive mental environment that instills confidence and self-belief. Athletes can utilize visualization to visualize themselves overcoming challenges, outperforming opponents, and standing atop the victory podium. This positive imagery stimulates the same neural pathways associated with actual success, thereby tricking the brain into believing in the athlete's capabilities.

Moreover, visualization can act as a powerful motivator. By engaging in mental rehearsals that elicit positive emotions and gratifying outcomes, athletes find renewed purpose and motivation to put in

the necessary effort and dedication required for success.
Visualization serves as a constant reminder of the rewards that await
them, nurturing a deep desire to push themselves beyond their
limits.

Overcoming Mental Barriers and Adversity

Sports competitions often entail high-pressure situations and
adversity. Athletes experience moments of anxiety, fear, and doubt,
which can significantly impact their performance. Visualization
offers a valuable means to overcome these mental barriers and excel
under challenging circumstances.

By mentally rehearsing scenarios that might induce fear or evoke
negative emotions, athletes can develop coping strategies and push
through their mental limitations. Through visualization, they can
train their minds to remain calm, composed, and resilient in the face
of adversity. This mental resilience can prove invaluable during
competitions, giving athletes an edge over their opponents.

Using Visualization as Complementary Training

Visualization should not be considered a replacement for physical
training; instead, it is a powerful tool that complements an athlete's
existing training regimen. To maximize the benefits of visualization,
athletes must integrate it into their overall routine, allotting specific
time for dedicated mental rehearsals.

Athletes can create a structured visualization practice by incorporating it into their pre-workout or pre-competition routine. By designating a few minutes before training or competition to engage in visualization exercises, athletes can effectively prime their minds and bodies for optimal performance.

The power of visualization in sports is an aspect often overlooked or underestimated. However, its impact on an athlete's performance, mindset, and overall success is profound. By incorporating visualization into their training regimens, athletes can enhance their focus, concentration, confidence, and mental resilience. Visualization allows athletes to prepare their minds for competitions, unleash hidden potential, and overcome mental barriers that may hinder their progress. Embracing the power of imagery not only supplements physical training but also empowers athletes to harness the boundless potential of their minds, unlocking a competitive advantage that sets them apart from the rest.

Mindfulness and Meditation for Athletes: Harnessing the present moment to improve performance

In the fast-paced world of sports, athletes are constantly driven to push their limits, seeking the edge that will elevate their performance above their competitors. While physical training, tactical strategies, and technical skills are vital components of athletic success, there is an often-overlooked aspect that can significantly impact an athlete's performance – the power of mindfulness and meditation. This chapter explores how athletes can harness the present moment through these practices to enhance their performance, both physically and mentally.

The Present Moment:

Athletes are accustomed to striving for future goals, relentlessly pursuing victory or success. However, in the process, they often forget the power of the present moment. Mindfulness and meditation techniques remind athletes that their performance is based on their ability to focus, remain fully engaged, and make split-second decisions – all of which occur in the present moment.

Understanding Mindfulness:

Mindfulness is the practice of intentionally bringing one's attention to the present moment, without judgment or attachment. By immersing themselves in the here and now, athletes can enhance their connection with their bodies and surroundings, allowing them to perform at their peak.

Benefits of Mindfulness in Athletics:

When athletes cultivate mindfulness, they experience numerous benefits that directly translate to improved performance. Firstly, mindfulness heightens body awareness, enabling athletes to sense even the slightest changes or tensions within their bodies. This heightened awareness facilitates injury prevention and allows for proactive correction of improper techniques.

Additionally, mindfulness enhances focus and concentration, enabling athletes to block out distractions and remain fully engaged in the task at hand. This laser-like focus not only improves performance during competition but also enhances practice sessions, ensuring that each repetition is executed with utmost concentration and intent.

Moreover, mindfulness helps athletes manage stress and anxiety, which are common byproducts of the competitive sports environment. By training their minds to remain calm and centered, athletes can navigate high-pressure situations with composure, improving decision-making and reducing performance-related stress.

Techniques for Incorporating Mindfulness:

Numerous techniques can help athletes incorporate mindfulness into their training routines. One such technique is breath awareness. Athletes can practice focusing solely on their breath, observing each inhalation and exhalation, thus grounding themselves in the present moment.

Another powerful technique is body scanning. This practice involves mentally scanning the body from head to toe, paying attention to any areas of tension or discomfort. By mindfully acknowledging these sensations, athletes can release any built-up tension and improve their overall physical well-being.

The Power of Meditation:

While mindfulness can be considered a general awareness practice, meditation takes the process a step further. Meditation involves setting aside dedicated time for deep introspection, reflection, and relaxation. By engaging in meditation practices specifically tailored to their athletic needs, athletes can enjoy a range of benefits that extend beyond their performance.

Enhancing Mental Clarity:

One of the primary benefits of meditation is its ability to sharpen mental clarity. Through regular practice, athletes can train their minds to stay focused, even in high-pressure situations. This heightened mental clarity allows athletes to make split-second decisions with precision, increasing their chances of success.

Strengthening Emotional Resilience:

Athletics can be an emotional rollercoaster, filled with triumphs and setbacks. Meditation equips athletes with the tools to navigate these emotional turbulences with poise. By cultivating emotional resilience, athletes can bounce back quickly from failures, maintain equanimity during success, and stay motivated throughout their journey.

Visualization and Affirmation:

Visualization and affirmation are two powerful meditation techniques that athletes can use to program their minds for success. By vividly imagining themselves achieving their goals or performing flawlessly, athletes create a mental blueprint for success. Coupled with affirmations and positive self-talk, these techniques build self-belief and reinforce a winning mindset.

Integrating Mindfulness and Meditation into Athletic Training:
For mindfulness and meditation to have a lasting impact on athletic performance, they must be integrated into an athlete's training regimen consistently. Athletes can allocate specific time slots for mindfulness and meditation practice, just as they do for physical training. These practices can be conducted individually or in guided sessions, depending on personal preference.

Moreover, coaches and trainers play a crucial role in promoting mindfulness and meditation among athletes. By introducing these practices in team exercises, warm-ups, or even recovery sessions, coaches can foster an environment that embraces the holistic development of their athletes, equipping them with mental tools to excel on and off the field.

In the competitive realm of athletics, athletes are always searching for that elusive edge that will set them apart from their rivals. Mindfulness and meditation provide a powerful avenue for athletes to access their untapped potential by harnessing the present moment. By integrating these practices into their training routines, athletes can enhance their physical abilities, sharpen their mental acuity, and cultivate emotional resilience, ultimately improving their performance and overall well-being as athletes.

Establishing Effective Pre-Game Rituals: Consistent practices to set oneself up for success.

Success in any endeavor, particularly in competitive sports, is often the result of discipline, focus, and a solid routine. Athletes who consistently perform at their peak recognize the importance of establishing effective pre-game rituals. These rituals not only serve as a physical and mental warm-up but also provide a sense of structure and familiarity that can calm nerves and boost confidence. In this chapter, we will explore the significance of pre-game rituals, the different types of rituals athletes can adopt, and how to customize them to suit individual needs and preferences. Step into the world of elite athletes as we uncover the secrets to their success.

The Power of Rituals:

Rituals are ingrained behaviors that provide a sense of order and predictability. They are deeply personal and often unique to each athlete, but their purpose remains consistent - to create a mental and physical state that optimizes performance. Developing pre-game rituals helps athletes prepare mentally, enhances focus, and ensures that they are physically ready for the challenges that lie ahead. Rituals can include a variety of activities such as visualizations, dynamic stretching, listening to music, or even specific superstitions. While the specific actions may vary, the underlying purpose remains the same - to create a sense of control, routine, and readiness.

Types of Pre-Game Rituals:

There are several types of pre-game rituals that athletes can utilize. Here, we will explore some of the most common ones and their benefits:

1. Mental Preparation:

Mental preparation rituals focus on getting into the right mindset for competition. Visualizations, affirmations, and meditation are commonly employed to enhance focus and confidence. These practices allow athletes to mentally rehearse their actions and envision success, which can have a profound impact on their performance. By mentally visualizing their strategy and envisioning a positive outcome, athletes can enhance their belief in achieving success.

2. Physical Warm-Up:

Physical warm-up rituals involve a series of activities aimed at preparing the body for optimal performance. Dynamic stretching, light cardio exercises, and mobility drills are a few examples of exercises athletes may include in their pre-game routines. These rituals not only help athletes prevent injuries but also promote blood flow, loosen muscles, and improve coordination. A thorough physical warm-up primes the body for the physical demands of the game.

3. Familiar Routine:

For some athletes, following a familiar routine provides a reassuring sense of familiarity. This ritual may involve specific activities such as wearing lucky socks, listening to a favorite playlist, or eating a particular meal before every competition. These acts help create a sense of familiarity and comfort, reducing anxiety and boosting confidence. The structure of a familiar routine can serve as a psychological anchor, enabling athletes to focus on the task at hand.

Customizing Your Pre-Game Rituals:

While it is essential to understand the purpose and types of pre-game rituals, it is equally important to customize these rituals to suit your individual needs and preferences. Here are some key factors to consider when crafting your own pre-game rituals:

1. Self-Reflection:

The first step in creating effective pre-game rituals is understanding what works best for you. Reflect on your previous experiences and identify the activities that have helped you perform your best. Consider the times when you felt most mentally focused and physically prepared. By understanding your strengths and weaknesses, you can tailor rituals that address your specific needs.

2. Experimentation:

Creating rituals is an ongoing process that requires experimentation. Try different activities and observe their impact on your performance. Keep a journal to record your experiences and evaluate which rituals positively contribute to your game. Stay open-minded and willing to adapt as your needs and circumstances change.

3. Consistency:

The power of pre-game rituals lies in their consistency. Regularly performing the same activities before every game trains your mind and body to associate these actions with optimal performance. Consistency also helps create a schedule that allows you to effectively manage your time, ensuring you have enough time for both physical and mental preparation.

4. Flexibility:

While consistency is crucial, it is equally important to remain flexible. Realize that some circumstances may prevent you from following your rituals precisely. For example, if you're competing in a different environment or facing unexpected time constraints, staying adaptable is key. Learn to adapt your rituals to fit the situation while maintaining the underlying purpose of mental and physical preparation.

5. Emotional Readiness:

Pre-game rituals are not only about the physical and mental aspects but also about emotional readiness. Recognize that emotions play a substantial role in performance. Incorporate activities that help you regulate your emotions, such as deep breathing exercises, listening to calming music, or engaging in positive self-talk. These practices will enable you to stay focused and composed under pressure.

The Stories Behind Success:

As we delve deeper into the world of pre-game rituals, it's fascinating to explore the rituals adopted by successful athletes in various sports. From small quirks to consistent routines, these rituals have often become synonymous with their success. Let's explore a few examples:

- Michael Jordan, the legendary basketball player, famously wore his college practice shorts under his NBA uniform in every game as a sign of respect and remembrance.

- Tennis champion Serena Williams meticulously bounces the ball five times before her first serve and twice before her second serve.

- Former MLB pitcher, Justin Verlander, has a strict pre-game routine that consists of eating the same meal before every start and listening to specific songs in a specific order to help him mentally prepare for the game.

These stories highlight the personal nature of pre-game rituals and their power in fostering consistency, focus, and confidence. Establishing effective pre-game rituals is a vital aspect of an athlete's preparation for success. By embracing rituals that encompass mental preparation, physical warm-up, and familiar routines, athletes set themselves up for optimal performance. Remember that rituals should be uniquely tailored to suit individual needs and preferences while remaining flexible in adapting to changing circumstances. As we explore the stories behind successful athletes and their rituals, it becomes clear that these practices go beyond superstition – they are the building blocks of greatness.

Coping Mechanisms for In-Game Stress: Techniques to manage stress in real-time

In the fast-paced world of gaming, stress can be an unavoidable side effect. Whether you're engaging in intense battles, racing against the clock, or trying to solve complex puzzles, the pressure to perform can sometimes become overwhelming. This chapter focuses on coping mechanisms that can be utilized in real-time to manage stress while playing games. By incorporating these techniques into your gaming routine, you can maintain a healthier mindset, enhance your performance, and ultimately derive more enjoyment from your gaming experience.

1. Breathing Techniques:

One of the most fundamental coping mechanisms for managing stress is to focus on your breath. Deep and controlled breathing can help regulate your heart rate and relax your body. In moments of high stress during gameplay, try taking a few slow, deep breaths. Inhale deeply through your nose, hold the breath briefly, and then exhale slowly through your mouth. This simple technique can provide an immediate sense of calm and help you regain your focus.

2. Developing a Positive Mindset:

In-game stress often arises from negative thoughts and self-doubt. By cultivating a positive mindset, you can counteract these harmful emotions. Practice self-affirmation by telling yourself positive statements such as "I can handle this challenge" or "I am improving with each attempt." Additionally, try to detach your self-worth from your gaming performance. Remember that even experienced players make mistakes and encounter difficulties. Embrace the learning process and view setbacks as valuable opportunities for growth.

3. Utilizing Time Management:

Time pressure is a common source of stress in many games. To effectively manage this stressor, employ time management strategies. Start by breaking down tasks into smaller, more manageable parts. Prioritize the most critical elements and allocate time accordingly. By efficiently utilizing the available time, you can maintain a sense of control and reduce the anxiety associated with impending deadlines. Remember, in gaming, as in life, managing time effectively is key to success.

4. Incorporating Physical Exercise:

Engaging in physical exercise while gaming may seem counterintuitive, but it can be surprisingly effective in alleviating stress. When faced with a challenging game situation, consider taking a short break to perform simple stretches or engage in a quick exercise routine. Physical activity increases blood flow to the brain, releasing endorphins and reducing stress levels. Such breaks can help clear your mind, improve focus, and allow you to return to the game with renewed energy and a refreshed perspective.

5. Applying Visualization Techniques:

Visualization is a powerful tool used by athletes, performers, and gamers alike. Before diving into a game, take a moment to visualize a successful outcome. Picture yourself skillfully navigating through challenging levels, achieving significant milestones, or triumphing over powerful adversaries. This mental rehearsal primes your mind for success, increases confidence, and reduces stress. Practice visualization regularly to create a positive outlook on your gaming sessions and improve your overall performance.

6. Employing Music Therapy:
Music has a profound impact on our emotions and can be a valuable resource for managing in-game stress. Experiment with different genres or soundtracks to find the music that relaxes and motivates you. Soft instrumental music or calming sounds from nature often work well to create a soothing gaming atmosphere. Alternatively, energetic and upbeat tunes can boost your adrenaline during intense gameplay, helping you to remain focused and energized. Customize your playlist according to your preferences and the specific game context to maximize its stress-reducing effects.

7. Seeking Social Support:
Gaming communities offer opportunities to connect with like-minded individuals who share similar experiences. During stressful gaming moments, reach out to friends, online teammates, or gaming communities for support. Sharing your frustrations, seeking advice, or simply venting about difficult challenges can provide a much-needed emotional release. Moreover, engaging in friendly competition or cooperative play with others can boost morale and

make the gaming experience more enjoyable. The power of community can help alleviate stress and create a sense of camaraderie within the gaming world.

8. Practicing Mindfulness:

Mindfulness is the practice of being fully present in the current moment, without judgment. Applying mindfulness techniques while gaming can help regulate stress and enhance overall performance. Start by focusing on the game's visuals, sounds, and your immediate actions, rather than getting caught up in future outcomes or past mistakes. Accept the imperfections and fluctuations in your performance without self-criticism, and instead, direct your attention back to the present. By cultivating mindfulness, you can navigate stressful gaming situations with a clear and composed mind.

Managing stress in real-time during intense gaming sessions is crucial to ensure both your mental well-being and gaming prowess. Incorporate these coping mechanisms - breathing techniques, developing a positive mindset, utilizing time management, incorporating physical exercise, applying visualization techniques, employing music therapy, seeking social support, and practicing mindfulness - to effectively manage stress while gaming. By doing so, you can maintain a healthier mindset, maximize your performance potential, and enhance your overall gaming experience.

Chapter 6: The Role of Support in Nurturing an Unyielding Spirit

In our journey through life, we all come face-to-face with challenges and obstacles that test the limits of our spirit. These moments of adversity have the power to break us, crush our dreams, and leave us feeling defeated. However, it is in these very moments that the role of support plays a crucial role in nurturing an unyielding spirit.

Support comes in various forms, from family and friends to mentors and communities. It is through these relationships that we find solace, encouragement, and the strength to keep going even when the odds seem insurmountable. In this chapter, we delve deep into understanding the significance of support and how it shapes our resilience and fortitude.

One cannot underestimate the power of human connection. It is a universal truth that we, as social beings, thrive on the support of others. When faced with challenges, having a support system that believes in our abilities and offers guidance can be the difference between surrendering to our circumstances and rising above them. In times of struggle, a simple word of encouragement or a helping hand can ignite a spark within us and push us to persevere.

Consider the story of Amelia, a budding entrepreneur, who faced countless rejections in her quest to secure funding for her groundbreaking business idea. Despite her unwavering determination, each rejection left her feeling hopeless and doubting her capabilities. It was only when she found a mentor who not only understood her vision but saw her potential that she regained her strength. This mentor believed in Amelia's abilities when she couldn't see it herself, providing her with the unwavering support she needed to carry on. With her mentor's support, Amelia went on to secure the necessary funding and transform her idea into a reality.

Support doesn't just have the power to restore our faith in ourselves; it can also serve as a source of motivation and inspiration. Surrounding ourselves with individuals who embody the qualities we aspire to have can serve as a constant reminder of what we are capable of achieving. These role models can offer guidance, share their experiences, and illuminate the path forward when we stumble in the darkness.

Rachel had always dreamed of becoming a professional dancer, but her journey was filled with self-doubt and fear of failure. It was her dance teacher, Ms. Johnson, who became her beacon of support. Ms. Johnson's unwavering belief in Rachel's talent and her unrelenting encouragement pushed Rachel to confront her fears and take the necessary risks to pursue her dreams. Ms. Johnson's constant support provided Rachel with the confidence she needed to audition for esteemed dance companies and eventually secure a spot in one of the world's most prestigious troupes.

Support goes beyond just belief and encouragement; it extends to providing practical assistance when needed. In times of hardship, having someone offer a helping hand can alleviate the burden we carry and give us the space to focus on overcoming the obstacle at hand. It is through this kind of support that we are empowered to tackle challenges head-on, with a renewed sense of hope and determination.

When Mark lost his job unexpectedly, he found himself grappling with financial insecurity and a sense of hopelessness. But his best friend, James, stepped in and offered Mark a place to stay until he got back on his feet. This act of kindness not only provided Mark with a roof over his head but also allowed him the mental space to search for new opportunities without the added stress of seeking immediate shelter. James's support allowed Mark to rebuild his life with greater resilience and gratitude.

Support, however, is a two-way street. Just as we rely on others for support, we must also be willing to extend it to those who need it. In cultivating relationships that foster mutual support, we build a community where everyone's unyielding spirit is not only celebrated but also nurtured. It is in these reciprocal bonds that we find strength, unity, and the power to face the world's challenges head-on.

The story of Jane exemplifies the power of reciprocal support. As a single mother, Jane found solace in a community of other single parents who faced similar struggles. Through their frequent gatherings, they created a network of support, sharing resources, babysitting responsibilities, and valuable advice. This support system helped Jane not only navigate the challenges of single parenthood but also encouraged her to pursue her education and advance her career, ensuring a better future for both herself and her children.

In nurturing an unyielding spirit, support stands as the cornerstone of our journey. It provides the scaffolding necessary to keep us standing tall through the storms of life. It is through the unwavering belief, encouragement, inspiration, and practical assistance of those around us that we are able to weather the toughest of adversities. So, let us remember the immense power that lies in support and strive to foster a community where unyielding spirits are nurtured and thrive.

The Significance of Mentorship in Sports: How experienced athletes can guide the younger generation

In the realm of sports, mentorship plays a crucial role in shaping the future of aspiring athletes. The journey from beginner to accomplished athlete is riddled with challenges, both physical and mental. The guidance and support of experienced athletes can pave the way for young athletes to overcome obstacles, develop necessary skills, and cultivate a winning mindset. In this chapter, we will explore the significance of mentorship in sports, highlighting how the wisdom of accomplished athletes can empower the younger generation.

Understanding Mentorship:

Mentorship, in the context of sports, refers to a relationship where an experienced athlete, the mentor, provides guidance, support, and knowledge to a younger athlete, the mentee. The mentor's role involves sharing practical advice, demonstrating skills, offering perspective, fostering a growth mindset, and teaching important life lessons both on and off the field. This form of mentorship is not limited to a single sport but can be found across various disciplines, from team sports like soccer and basketball to individual sports such as tennis and gymnastics.

Benefits of Mentorship for Young Athletes:

1. Skill Development: One of the primary advantages of mentorship is the accelerated skill development it offers to young athletes. An experienced mentor can identify areas of improvement, provide specific feedback, and teach techniques that have proven successful through their own experiences. This not only helps the mentee refine their skills but also allows them to avoid common mistakes and shortcuts, ensuring a solid foundation for their athletic journey.

2. Mental Fortitude: Sports can be mentally challenging, testing an athlete's resilience and determination. Mentors act as a source of motivation, instilling mental toughness in their mentees. By sharing their personal stories of overcoming adversity, mentors inspire young athletes to persevere during tough times, teaching them to bounce back from failures, and maintain a positive mindset towards their goals.

3. Emotional Support: Being a young athlete often comes with emotional highs and lows. Mentors provide a safe space for mentees to openly express their fears, doubts, and insecurities. By empathizing with the mentee's struggles, the mentor can offer guidance, reassurance, and constructive advice, ultimately helping the athlete navigate the emotional roller coaster that accompanies the pursuit of excellence.

4. Personal Growth: A mentor's influence extends far beyond the sports arena. Through mentorship, young athletes develop critical

life skills such as discipline, time management, teamwork, and goal-setting. These qualities not only contribute to their success in sports but also serve as valuable tools for their future endeavors, both inside and outside of athletics.

The Role of Mentors:

1. Sharing Knowledge: One of the fundamental responsibilities of a mentor is to share their knowledge and expertise with their mentees. This includes demonstrating essential techniques, teaching game tactics, and imparting strategic insights gained from years of experience. A strong mentor-mentee relationship is built on effective communication, where the mentor is not only seen as a teacher but also a guide and advisor.

2. Setting Goals: Mentors play a vital role in helping young athletes define their goals and develop a roadmap to achieve them. By setting realistic yet challenging objectives, mentors instill a sense of purpose and direction in their mentees. They assist in breaking down long-term goals into smaller, manageable steps, ensuring continuous progress and growth throughout the athlete's journey.

3. Leading by Example: Perhaps the most powerful aspect of mentorship is the mentor's ability to lead by example. Accomplished athletes can serve as living proof that success is attainable through hard work, discipline, dedication, and resilience. By embodying these qualities, mentors inspire their mentees to adopt the same values and behaviors, pushing them to reach their full potential.

4. Providing Support: Mentors act as a support system for young athletes, offering encouragement, motivation, and a shoulder to lean on during challenging times. They provide constructive feedback while creating an environment of trust and respect. Additionally, mentors help their mentees build resilience and coping mechanisms to deal with failures and setbacks, ultimately shaping them into well-rounded individuals.

The Impact of Mentorship:

The impact of mentorship in sports can be far-reaching, benefiting both the individual athlete and the entire sports community. Let us explore how mentorship affects various aspects of the sports world.

1. Athletic Success: The guidance and support received from mentors significantly increase the chances of young athletes achieving their athletic goals. Whether it be making a school team, competing at the elite level, or even representing their country, mentorship plays a critical role in developing the skills, mindset, and determination required to succeed in sports.

2. Positive Sports Culture: Mentorship fosters a positive sports culture by promoting sportsmanship, teamwork, and camaraderie among athletes. Through mentorship, young athletes learn the importance of fair play, respect for opponents, and valuing the overall experience of the game over winning at all costs. These values translate into a healthier and more enjoyable sporting

environment for all participants.

3. Legacy of Knowledge: Mentorship ensures the wisdom and knowledge acquired by experienced athletes are passed down to the younger generation. This legacy helps preserve valuable lessons, strategies, and techniques that may have taken a lifetime to master. By transmitting these lessons, mentors contribute to the growth and evolution of the sport itself.

The significance of mentorship in sports cannot be overstated. It acts as a bridge connecting the accomplishments and experiences of seasoned athletes with the aspirations and dreams of the younger generation. Through mentorship, young athletes can tap into the wealth of knowledge, guidance, and support that mentors bring to the table. This symbiotic relationship not only shapes individual athletes but also leaves an enduring imprint on the sporting community as a whole. Whether through skill development, mental fortitude, emotional support, or personal growth, mentorship is a catalyst for success in sports and beyond.

Building a Supportive Team Environment: The importance of mutual encouragement and trust

In any organization or team, individuals come together with unique skills and abilities to achieve a common goal. However, a supportive team environment is crucial for harnessing the collective potential of each team member. It lays the foundation for open communication, collaboration, and continuous improvement. Central to this productive environment are two vital elements: mutual encouragement and trust. This chapter delves into the significance of these components and explores how they foster a positive team culture.

The Power of Mutual Encouragement

Encouragement is a powerful tool that sparks motivation and inspires individuals to strive for excellence. When team members actively support and uplift each other, the entire team benefits. Mutual encouragement creates an atmosphere of positivity, building resilience and determination within the team.

1. Boosting Morale

Mutual encouragement goes beyond individual recognition; it

creates a collective spirit that lifts the morale of the entire team. By acknowledging each team member's efforts and successes, individuals feel valued and appreciated. As a result, their commitment towards the team's objectives increases, leading to enhanced productivity and engagement.

2. Building Confidence

Supportive team environments foster a sense of psychological safety, allowing individuals to take risks without the fear of judgment or failure. When team members encourage one another, they help build confidence. By believing in each other's abilities, team members can step out of their comfort zones, unlocking their full potential.

3. Strengthening Collaboration

When team members encourage each other, they focus on developing strategic collaborations. The exchange of ideas and expertise becomes more seamless, enabling effective problem-solving and innovation. When individuals trust that their suggestions will be met with support and respect, they feel comfortable sharing their perspectives, ultimately leading to better decision-making and creative solutions.

The Significance of Trust

Trust forms the bedrock of any successful team environment. It promotes open and honest communication, encourages risk-taking, and establishes a sense of psychological safety among team members. Building trust takes time and effort, but the rewards are immeasurable.

1. Enhancing Communication

In a team environment, trust encourages open and transparent communication. Individuals feel comfortable expressing their thoughts, concerns, and ideas without fear of reprisal. This enables teams to exchange information freely, improving task comprehension, minimizing misunderstandings, and enhancing overall team performance.

2. Fostering Collaboration and Cooperation

Trust plays a critical role in fostering collaboration and cooperation within a team. When team members trust each other's intentions and capabilities, they are more likely to collaborate effectively, respecting each other's contributions. Trust dismantles barriers, enhances team cohesion, and facilitates a sense of collective responsibility towards shared objectives.

3. Promoting Risk-Taking and Innovation

Trust allows individuals to take risks and think creatively, unafraid of making mistakes. When team members have confidence in each other, they are more likely to experiment with new ideas, leading to innovation. Trust empowers teams to challenge the status quo, explore uncharted territories, and find groundbreaking solutions to complex problems.

Building a Supportive Team Environment

Creating a supportive team environment requires intentional and ongoing efforts. Here are some strategies to foster mutual encouragement and trust within your team:

1. Lead by Example

Leadership plays a crucial role in cultivating a supportive team environment. As a leader, it is vital to lead by example and encourage positive behavior among team members. By demonstrating trust, giving recognition, and providing constructive feedback, leaders set the tone for a supportive atmosphere.

2. Foster Communication Channels

Establishing effective communication channels is essential for team members to connect and engage. Encourage regular team meetings, both virtually and in-person, to promote open dialogue.

Furthermore, provide opportunities for one-on-one conversations to build more personal connections, ensuring that every team member feels heard and valued.

3. Encourage Collaboration and Knowledge Sharing

Promote a culture of collaboration by creating platforms that facilitate knowledge sharing and cross-functional teamwork. Encourage the exchange of best practices, lessons learned, and promote the utilization of diverse perspectives within the team. This will not only enhance team performance but also nurture an environment of continuous learning.

4. Celebrate Successes and Learn from Failures

Keep the team motivated and engaged by celebrating individual and team achievements. Recognize the efforts of each team member and acknowledge their contributions. Conversely, when failures occur, approach them as learning opportunities rather than casting blame. Emphasize collective growth and encourage team members to share lessons learned from setbacks.

5. Establish Trust-Building Activities

Engage in trust-building activities that foster camaraderie and familiarity among team members. Organize team-building exercises, both within and outside the workplace, to encourage interaction, collaboration, and trust. Such activities help build relationships based on shared experiences and reinforce mutual understanding.

In a supportive team environment, mutual encouragement and trust are the key ingredients that drive success. By promoting a positive atmosphere where team members uplift and inspire each other, organizations can harness the collective capabilities of their teams. Trust, on the other hand, establishes an open and honest communication channel that fuels collaboration and innovation. By implementing the strategies outlined in this chapter, leaders can build teams that thrive, celebrate successes, navigate challenges, and create an environment conducive to continuous growth and achievement.

Parental Influence on an Athlete's Mental State: Understanding the impact of parents' attitudes

In the world of sports, the impact of parents on an athlete's life is undeniable. From an early age, parents play a pivotal role in nurturing their child's athletic potential and shaping their mental state. While the physical aspect of sports receives much attention, it is equally important to understand the profound influence parents have on the psychological well-being of young athletes. This chapter aims to delve into the intricate dynamics between parents and athletes and explore the ways in which parental attitudes can either foster or hinder their child's development in the sporting arena.

Fostering a Positive Athletic Environment:

The initial steps towards understanding the impact of parental influence on an athlete's mental state lie in recognizing the significance of a positive athletic environment. Parents who actively promote positivity, support, and encouragement create an atmosphere that can empower their child's athletic journey. By offering unconditional love, showing empathy, and maintaining open communication, parents establish a foundation built on trust and understanding.

One of the primary roles parents play is that of a motivator. They can significantly impact an athlete's mental state by instilling a belief in their capabilities. Through positive reinforcement and constructive feedback, parents can boost their child's self-confidence, setting the stage for a resilient athlete who can withstand challenges both on and off the field. When parents express belief in their child's abilities, it fosters a sense of validation and creates an internal drive, pushing the athlete to strive for excellence.

Understanding the Power of Words:

While it is crucial for parents to offer support, it is equally important to understand the power of their words. Often unintentionally, parents may slip into patterns of communication that inadvertently undermine their child's mental well-being. Excessive criticism, unrealistic expectations, or ridicule can create significant negative impacts on the athlete's self-esteem and self-image.

Research has shown that negative comments or overly harsh feedback can contribute to anxiety, performance anxiety, and reduced motivation in young athletes. Therefore, parents must learn how to strike a balance between providing guidance and maintaining a nurturing environment. Constructive criticism should be relayed in a way that focuses on improvement rather than tearing down the athlete's self-worth.

Maintaining Boundaries:

The involvement of parents in their child's athletic journey can be a double-edged sword. While supportive involvement is beneficial, excessive or overbearing behavior can hinder the athlete's mental state. It is essential for parents to recognize the significance of maintaining boundaries and allowing their child's sport to be primarily their own domain.

When parents exert too much control or pressure over their child's sporting activities, it can lead to burnout and a loss of enjoyment. Athletes may feel overwhelmed by parental expectations, resulting in decreased interest and motivation. By allowing their child to experience autonomy and ownership over their athletic pursuits, parents enable their growth as independent individuals both on and off the field.

Modeling Healthy Behavior:

The influence of parental behavior extends beyond what is said. Parents serve as role models for their children, and their own attitudes towards sports can shape the way their child perceives and engages with athletics. Children look up to their parents and often emulate their actions, both in sports and in life. Therefore, by embodying healthy behavior, parents can positively influence their child's mental state and attitude towards sports.
Parents who exhibit resilience in the face of challenges, demonstrate good sportsmanship, and emphasize the importance of a balanced

life serve as powerful examples to their young athletes. When children witness their parents handling wins and losses with grace, they learn to approach their sporting endeavors with a healthy perspective, valuing growth and personal development above all else.

Navigating the Competitive Landscape:

In an increasingly competitive athletics landscape, parents must navigate the fine line between supporting their child's ambitions and fostering an unhealthy obsession with winning. While it is natural to want the best for their child, parents must understand that placing excessive emphasis on winning can be detrimental to an athlete's mental state.

The fear of disappointing parents or not meeting their expectations can lead to heightened anxiety and performance-related stress. As parents, it is important to focus on the process of improvement, celebrating achievements and milestones along the way, rather than solely fixating on the outcome. By fostering a growth mindset, parents can equip their child to face challenges head-on, embrace failures as learning opportunities, and develop a love for the game that transcends wins and losses.

Seeking Professional Help for Mental Challenges: Emphasizing the role of sports psychologists

The field of sports psychology has gained significant recognition and importance over the years. Athletes are increasingly confronted with mental challenges that can impact their performance on and off the field. In light of this, seeking professional help has become crucial to ensure optimal mental health and performance enhancement. This chapter will delve into the significance of professional assistance for athletes grappling with mental challenges, with a special emphasis on the role of sports psychologists.

Understanding Mental Challenges in Athletes

Athletes face a myriad of mental challenges throughout their careers, which can significantly impact their well-being and performance. Stress, anxiety, depression, and burnout are some of the most common mental challenges that athletes encounter. Furthermore, they may also experience issues related to self-confidence, focus, motivation, and emotional regulation. These mental challenges can affect an athlete's ability to make sound decisions, stay motivated, and maintain a healthy mindset both in training and during competitions.

Recognizing the Importance of Professional Help

In the past, mental health issues among athletes were often disregarded or considered secondary to physical performance. However, the tide has turned, and athletes are now encouraged to seek professional help for the betterment of their mental well-being. Just as athletes rely on coaches, trainers, and nutritionists to optimize their physical performance, the addition of a sports psychologist to the support team can be equally essential.

Sports Psychologists: The Key to Mental Strength

Sports psychologists specialize in understanding athletes' mental challenges and developing effective strategies to help them overcome obstacles and enhance performance. These professionals not only have a deep understanding of psychology but also possess specialized knowledge of the unique pressures, stressors, and demands faced by athletes.

Role of Sports Psychologists in Athletes' Lives

1. Assessing and Managing Mental Health Issues: Sports psychologists play a crucial role in assessing and managing mental health issues in athletes. Through careful evaluation, they can identify psychological challenges interfering with an athlete's performance and overall well-being. They then work collaboratively

with the athletes to develop personalized treatment plans, which may involve various therapeutic techniques, including cognitive-behavioral therapy (CBT), mindfulness practices, and visualization exercises.

2. Building Mental Resilience: Mental resilience is vital for athletes as it helps them cope with setbacks, pressure, and adversity. Sports psychologists assist athletes in developing mental resilience by teaching them techniques to regulate their emotions, manage stress, and stay focused amidst distractions. By working on mental resilience, athletes can enhance their ability to bounce back from failures, perform under pressure, and maintain a positive mindset.

3. Performance Enhancement: Sports psychologists are well-equipped to help athletes enhance their performance on the field. They use a range of psychological strategies tailored to individual athletes' needs, such as goal-setting, imagery rehearsal, attention and concentration strategies, and psychophysiological techniques. By incorporating these techniques into their training regimens, athletes can maximize their potential and optimize their performance when it matters the most.

4. Team Dynamics and Communication: In team sports, collaboration and effective communication are crucial. Sports psychologists work with athletes to improve their communication skills, facilitate healthy team dynamics, and foster a supportive and cohesive team environment. By enhancing interpersonal skills, athletes can build

stronger relationships with their teammates, coaches, and support staff, leading to improved overall team performance.

5. Life Beyond Sport: Athletes often struggle with transitioning out of their sports careers into life beyond the field. Sports psychologists offer support during this transitional phase, helping athletes navigate challenges such as identity crises, post-career depression, and the search for new passions and goals. By addressing these transitional challenges head-on, sports psychologists can assist athletes in finding fulfillment and success in their post-sports lives.

In today's increasingly competitive and demanding world of sports, the significance of mental health and well-being cannot be understated. Athletes who seek professional help from sports psychologists gain access to a range of services aimed at managing mental challenges and enhancing performance. By utilizing the expertise of these specialists, athletes are better equipped to cope with adversity, build mental resilience, maximize their performance, and successfully transition to life beyond sports. In the subsequent chapters, we will discuss case studies and testimonials of athletes who have sought professional help and experienced remarkable transformations under the guidance of sports psychologists.

Chapter 7: The Long-Term Rewards of Mental Resilience

Life is full of challenges, obstacles, and setbacks that can often leave us feeling overwhelmed and defeated. However, it is our ability to bounce back from adversity that truly determines our success and happiness in the long run. In Chapter 7 of our book, "The Power of Resilience," we delve into the concept of mental resilience and explore the incredible long-term rewards it can offer. From improved mental health to enhanced relationships and career success, mental resilience is a skill worth cultivating.

Navigating Life's Challenges

Life is unpredictable, and no matter how well we plan, unexpected challenges will inevitably arise. Mental resilience allows us to approach these challenges with a healthy and constructive mindset, enabling us to find solutions, learn from our experiences, and grow stronger. When faced with a setback, mentally resilient individuals view it as a temporary obstacle rather than a permanent roadblock. They are able to remain focused, level-headed, and optimistic, which empowers them to tackle challenges head-on.

Mental Health and Well-being

One of the most significant long-term rewards of mental resilience is improved mental health and overall well-being. Being mentally resilient doesn't mean we won't experience negative emotions or hardships. Instead, it means that we possess the tools and attitudes necessary to cope with and overcome these difficulties effectively. Research has consistently shown that individuals with high levels of resilience report lower levels of depression, anxiety, and stress. They are better equipped to manage their emotions, regulate stress, and maintain a positive outlook on life even during tough times.

Building Strong Relationships

Strong and meaningful connections with others are essential for our overall well-being and happiness. However, relationships are not immune to challenges, conflicts, and disagreements. Mental resilience plays a crucial role in maintaining healthy relationships, as it allows us to navigate conflicts without becoming deeply affected or overwhelmed. Resilient individuals possess excellent communication skills, empathy, and the ability to manage their emotions. These skills enable them to listen to others, understand their perspectives, and find constructive solutions to conflicts. Ultimately, mental resilience strengthens relationships, fosters trust, and deepens emotional bonds.

Career Success

In today's highly competitive world, mental resilience is a valuable asset that can significantly impact our career success. Resilient individuals are better equipped to handle the inevitable stressors and setbacks that come with professional life. Through setbacks, failures, and rejections, they remain persistent and focused on their goals. Mental resilience empowers us to adapt to changes, embrace challenges as growth opportunities, and maintain a positive attitude in the face of adversities. Employers value individuals who possess mental resilience as they are more likely to take on leadership roles, display innovative thinking, and excel in dynamic work environments.

Achieving Personal Growth and Fulfillment

Life is a journey of personal growth, and mental resilience serves as an essential tool for continuous self-improvement. Resilient individuals embrace challenges as opportunities for growth rather than setbacks. They have a growth mindset and are always open to learning from failures and mistakes. Mental resilience empowers individuals to reflect on their experiences, identify areas for improvement, and take the necessary steps to develop their skills and abilities. By leveraging their resilience, individuals can unlock their full potential, achieve personal goals, and experience a deep sense of fulfillment in all aspects of life.

Cultivating Mental Resilience

While some individuals may possess a natural inclination towards mental resilience, it is also a skill that can be developed and cultivated over time. Here are some strategies to enhance mental resilience:

1. Building a strong support network: Surround yourself with positive and supportive individuals who uplift you during challenging times.

2. Building self-awareness: Understand your emotions, strengths, and weaknesses to better navigate stressful situations.

3. Practicing mindfulness: Engage in mindfulness exercises or meditation to enhance self-regulation skills and promote mental clarity.

4. Developing problem-solving skills: Focus on finding solutions rather than dwelling on problems. Break down challenges into manageable steps and take action.

5. Cultivating positivity: Practice gratitude, positive self-talk, and seek out silver linings in challenging situations.

6. Embracing failure: Shift your perspective on failure, seeing it as a necessary stepping stone towards success. Learn from your mistakes and bounce back stronger.

Beyond the Field: Life Skills from Sports: How mental toughness benefits life outside of sports

Sports have always been recognized for their physical benefits, but they offer much more than just physical fitness. Engaging in sports cultivates mental toughness, which plays a vital role in an athlete's success on the field. However, mental toughness is not limited to the boundaries of the sports arena. It extends far beyond, benefiting athletes in their personal and professional lives. In this chapter, we will explore the various ways in which mental toughness acquired through sports can positively impact an individual's life beyond the field.

Building Resilience:

One of the key components of mental toughness is resilience - the ability to bounce back from failure, setbacks, and challenges. Athletes face numerous obstacles on their journey to success, often experiencing defeat and disappointment along the way. This constant exposure to adversity hones their resilience, enabling them to develop a positive mindset and the ability to overcome challenges in all aspects of life.

Outside of sports, resilience is an essential life skill. It helps individuals navigate through difficult situations, such as career setbacks, personal losses, or financial hardships. By drawing from their experiences on the field, individuals with mental toughness are better equipped to withstand hardships and bounce back stronger than before, irrespective of the domain.

Goal Setting and Perseverance:

Sports provide athletes with an invaluable platform to set and pursue goals. Athletes are often required to set both short-term and long-term goals, which they work relentlessly to achieve. This process ingrains a strong sense of perseverance and drive within athletes, propelling them to strive for success. Not only do they learn how to set realistic and achievable goals, but they also develop the determination required to stay committed and focused on their objectives.

Transferring this skill to everyday life, individuals with mental toughness display exceptional goal setting abilities. They have the discipline and determination necessary to outline their aspirations and put in the effort required to achieve them. Whether it is establishing career objectives, personal milestones, or even improving their mental and physical well-being, individuals with mental toughness possess the tools to overcome obstacles and keep their eyes on the prize.

Effective Stress Management:

Sports can be highly demanding, both physically and mentally. Athletes often find themselves in high-pressure situations, such as crucial competitions or challenging teammates. To excel in such situations, athletes develop effective stress management techniques, which allow them to perform at their best regardless of the circumstances. Whether it is maintaining composure under pressure, staying focused amidst distractions, or controlling their emotions, athletes are adept at managing stress in a healthy and productive manner.

Outside of sports, stress is an inevitable part of life. However, individuals with mental toughness bring their well-honed stress management skills to the table. They have the ability to handle stressful situations with composure, keeping a clear mind to make rational decisions. Such individuals are less likely to succumb to the negative effects of stress and are more likely to find constructive ways to overcome challenges rather than becoming overwhelmed by them.

Enhanced Time Management:

Sports demand rigorous training schedules, balancing academics (if young athletes) or work (for adults), and maintaining a healthy personal life. Athletes with mental toughness are proficient in time management, efficiently organizing their days to squeeze in training, studying, and leisure activities. They understand the value of discipline, planning, and setting priorities, which allows them to maximize productivity and achieve their desired outcomes.

In daily life, time management is an indispensable skill that directly impacts an individual's productivity, success, and overall well-being. Individuals with mental toughness excel in managing their time, allowing them to balance their personal and professional commitments effectively. By utilizing their time efficiently, they can devote ample attention to various aspects of their lives and ensure they achieve their goals in a holistic manner.

Improved Communication and Teamwork:

One cannot thrive in sports without effective communication and teamwork. Athletes understand the importance of building relationships, collaborating with teammates, and effectively communicating strategies and ideas. A crucial aspect of mental toughness involves forging strong connections with teammates, coaches, and support staff, creating a sense of unity and shared goals.

Outside of sports, effective communication and teamwork skills enable individuals to excel in their personal and professional relationships. Individuals with mental toughness possess the ability to understand diverse perspectives, collaborate efficiently, and communicate their thoughts clearly. These skills foster strong relationships, enhance team dynamics, and contribute to success in various realms of life.

Mental toughness acquired through sports transcends the confines of the playing field, positively impacting an individual's life on multiple levels. Resilience, goal setting, effective stress management, time management, improved communication, and teamwork are just a few examples of the extensive benefits that mental toughness brings beyond sports.

Cultivating mental toughness equips individuals with a robust framework to overcome adversity, achieve their goals, and become well-rounded individuals capable of navigating life's challenges.

Handling Success and Failure Gracefully: Navigating the highs and lows with an even keel

Success and failure are two sides of the same coin that we inevitably encounter on our journey through life. Each one has the power to reshape us, challenging our character and resilience. In this chapter, we explore the art of handling success and failure gracefully, learning how to navigate the highs and lows with an even keel.

The Nature of Success and Failure

Before diving deeper into our discussion, it is crucial to understand the nature of success and failure. Success is often perceived as the accomplishment of a goal or the attainment of a desirable outcome, while failure, on the other hand, is viewed as falling short of achieving that goal or experiencing an undesired outcome.

However, it is essential to challenge these simplistic definitions and instead embrace a more nuanced understanding of success and failure. Success should not be solely measured by external achievements but should also encompass personal growth, happiness, and fulfillment. Conversely, failure should not be seen as an indictment of our worth but as an opportunity for learning and self-improvement.

The Dangers of Success

At first glance, success might seem like an unquestionably positive outcome. However, it brings with it unique challenges and risks that can undermine our personal and professional growth if not handled with care.

One danger of success is complacency. When we achieve a certain level of success, it is easy to become comfortable and to settle for the status quo. We may start taking things for granted or get stuck in our comfort zone, inhibiting our motivation for further growth and improvement.

Another peril of success is the potential for ego inflation. As our achievements accumulate, we may start to perceive ourselves as invulnerable or superior to others. This inflated ego can cloud our judgment, hinder collaboration, and create barriers that hinder our continuous development.

Additionally, success can breed unrealistic expectations and pressure. Once we taste success, whether it be in our career, relationships, or personal endeavors, we may feel the need to constantly seek validation from others. This constant pressure to maintain success can lead to burnout, anxiety, and the loss of our authentic selves.

Navigating Success with Grace

To handle success gracefully, it is crucial to cultivate self-awareness and maintain a humble perspective. Here are some strategies to help you navigate the highs of success without losing yourself:

1. Practice Gratitude: Stay grounded by acknowledging and appreciating the people, opportunities, and circumstances that contributed to your success. Cultivating gratitude not only keeps your ego in check but also promotes feelings of contentment and happiness.

2. Embrace Continuous Growth: Instead of resting on your laurels, strive for continuous self-improvement and growth. Success should not be the end goal but rather a stepping stone towards new challenges and aspirations.

3. Foster Collaboration: Surround yourself with diverse perspectives and collaborate with others. Let go of the need to be the sole contributor. Harness the power of teamwork, as it not only enhances creativity and innovation but also keeps your ego in check.

4. Stay Authentic: Success may tempt you to conform to societal expectations or to present a false version of yourself. Stay true to your values, passions, and beliefs. Authenticity fosters genuine connections and leads to long-lasting fulfillment.

Deconstructing Failure

Failure, often seen as the opposite of success, carries its own set of challenges and opportunities. While it can be disheartening and discouraging, failure is an inevitable part of life and can be a powerful catalyst for personal growth and resilience.

One common misconception surrounding failure is the belief that it defines us. When we fail, we may internalize the experience as a reflection of our abilities or self-worth. It is crucial to challenge this notion and understand that failure is merely a temporary setback—a stepping stone on the path to success.

Failure is also an excellent teacher that highlights areas for improvement and growth. Through failure, we gain valuable wisdom and lessons that can be applied in future endeavors. Embracing failure as a natural part of life's journey allows for self-reflection, learning, and the development of a growth mindset.

Navigating Failure with Resilience

To handle failure gracefully and navigate its lows, it is essential to cultivate resilience and embrace the following strategies:

1. Practice Self-Compassion: Instead of berating yourself when you fail, offer kindness and understanding. Treat yourself as you would a dear friend, acknowledging that failure is a part of the human experience.

2. Reframe Failure: Rather than seeing failure as a roadblock, reframe it as a necessary stepping stone to success. Embrace a growth mindset, viewing failure as an opportunity for learning, self-improvement, and personal evolution.

3. Seek Support: Reach out to your support network during times of failure. Share your experiences and emotions with trusted friends, family, or mentors who can provide guidance, perspective, and encouragement.

4. Set Realistic Expectations: Avoid setting unrealistic expectations that may perpetuate a fear of failure. Recognize that success is rarely linear, and setbacks are an inherent part of the journey.

Handling success and failure gracefully requires a delicate balance of self-awareness, humility, and resilience. Celebrate your achievements with gratitude and keep striving for growth, even when success comes knocking at your door. Similarly, embrace failure as a stepping stone towards success, learning from each experience with resilience and compassion. By navigating the highs and lows with an even keel, you can lead a more fulfilling and purposeful life, embracing the journey's transformative power.

Continuous Evolution of the Athletic Mind: The journey of mental growth never stops

In the pursuit of athletic excellence, it is often said that the greatest battle is fought within the mind. While physical prowess and technical skills are undoubtedly crucial, the athletic mind plays a pivotal role in determining an athlete's success. This chapter explores the concept of continuous evolution of the athletic mind, emphasizing that the journey of mental growth is an ongoing process that never truly ends. The remarkable stories of athletes who have dedicated their lives to this pursuit will serve as an inspiration for all aspiring athletes seeking to unlock the full potential of their minds.

Section 1: The Athletic Mindset

1.1 Breaking the Mental Barriers

The seeds of mental growth are planted when athletes confront and conquer their own self-imposed limitations. Everyday obstacles, self-doubt, and fear breed a mindset that hinders progress. The first step towards continuous evolution lies in challenging these mental barriers head-on. Athletes must develop strategies to overcome fear, embrace failure as a stepping stone, and cultivate a positive mindset that perseveres through adversity.

1.2 The Power of Visualization

Visualization is a potent tool used by athletes to enhance their performance. It involves mentally rehearsing every aspect of a desired outcome, creating a blueprint in the mind that guides the body. By harnessing the power of visualization and incorporating it into their training routines, athletes can sculpt their minds to align with their athletic aspirations. This chapter will explore various visualization techniques used by successful athletes and their impact on mental growth.

Section 2: Mental Resilience

2.1 Embracing the Growth Mindset

The growth mindset is an essential quality adopted by champions. Athletes need to believe in their capacity to grow and improve, constantly seeking new challenges and embracing failure as an opportunity for growth. Cultivating a growth mindset allows athletes to approach setbacks with resilience, using them as springboards for future success. This section will delve into the mindset shifts required to develop mental resilience and explain how they contribute to continuous mental growth.

2.2 Mastering the Art of Focus

The ability to maintain unwavering focus amidst distractions is a hallmark of an evolved athletic mind. Athletes who perfect their focus not only perform better, but they also experience enhanced mental growth. This section will explore the importance of training focus, techniques for improving concentration, and the neuroscience behind attention control. The stories of athletes who have harnessed this skill to unlock their full potential will inspire readers to do the same.

Section 3: Overcoming Mental Roadblocks

3.1 Battling Performance Anxiety

Performance anxiety is a common mental roadblock that prevents athletes from realizing their true potential. Fear of failure, pressure to perform, and self-doubt can cripple even the most gifted individuals. This chapter will delve into effective strategies to overcome performance anxiety, providing practical advice that athletes can implement to conquer their inner fears and channel their nervous energy in a positive manner.

3.2 Managing Stress and Burnout

The pursuit of athletic excellence is known to exact a toll on an athlete's mental and emotional well-being. The pressure to succeed, constant demands, and intense training regimens can lead to stress and burnout. This section explores holistic approaches to managing stress and nurturing mental health. It offers practical advice on setting boundaries, adopting self-care practices, and promoting mental equilibrium, urging athletes to prioritize their well-being as a fundamental aspect of continuous mental growth.

Section 4: The Role of Mentors and Support Systems

4.1 Unlocking the Power of Mentorship

Mentors play an indispensable role in an athlete's journey of mental growth. They offer guidance, share wisdom, and provide a safe space for athletes to explore their vulnerabilities. This chapter will shed light on the importance of mentor relationships, revealing the transformative impact they can have on an athlete's mindset. Stories of athletes who have thrived under the guidance of their mentors will exemplify the value of this pivotal connection.

4.2 Strengthening Support Systems

Behind every successful athlete is a strong support system comprising coaches, teammates, family, and friends. They provide encouragement, motivation, and a collective belief in an athlete's potential. This section delves into the ways athletes can cultivate a support system that fosters their mental growth. It highlights the significance of healthy relationships, effective communication, and the environment in shaping the athletic mind.